THE ILIAD

Homer

EDITORIAL DIRECTOR Justin Kestler
EXECUTIVE EDITOR Ben Florman

SERIES EDITORS Boomie Aglietti, John Crowther, Justin Kestler
PRODUCTION Christian Lorentzen

WRITERS Brian Phillips, James Hunter
EDITORS Katie Mannheimer, Boomie Aglietti, John Crowther, Justin Kestler

This edition published by Spark Publishing

Spark Publishing
A Division of SparkNotes LLC
120 Fifth Avenue, 8th Floor
New York, NY 10011

02 03 04 05 SN 9 8 7 6 5 4 3

Please send all comments and questions or report errors to
feedback@sparknotes.com.

Library of Congress information available upon request

Printed and bound in the United States

RRD-C

ISBN 1-58663-371-6

Introduction: Stopping to Buy Sparknotes on a Snowy Evening

Whose words these are you *think* you know.
Your paper's due tomorrow, though;
We're glad to see you stopping here
To get some help before you go.

Lost your course? You'll find it here.
Face tests and essays without fear.
Between the words, good grades at stake:
Get great results throughout the year.

Once school bells caused your heart to quake
As teachers circled each mistake.
Use SparkNotes and no longer weep,
Ace every single test you take.

Yes, books are lovely, dark, and deep,
But only what you grasp you keep,
With hours to go before you sleep,
With hours to go before you sleep.

Contents

CONTEXT 1
 THE AFTERMATH OF THE ILIAD 3

PLOT OVERVIEW 7

CHARACTER LIST 9
 THE ACHAEANS (ALSO CALLED
  THE "ARGIVES" OR "DANAANS") 9
 THE TROJANS 11
 THE GODS AND IMMORTALS 13

ANALYSIS OF MAJOR CHARACTERS 15
 ACHILLES 15
 AGAMEMNON 16
 HECTOR 16

THEMES, MOTIFS & SYMBOLS 19
 THE GLORY OF WAR 19
 MILITARY GLORY OVER FAMILY LIFE 20
 THE IMPERMANENCE OF HUMAN LIFE
  AND ITS CREATIONS 20
 ARMOR 21
 BURIAL 21
 FIRE 22
 THE ACHAEAN SHIPS 22
 THE SHIELD OF ACHILLES 23

SUMMARY & ANALYSIS   25
    BOOK 1   25
    BOOK 2   28
    BOOKS 3–4   30
    BOOKS 5–6   33
    BOOKS 7–8   36
    BOOKS 9–10   39
    BOOKS 11–12   42
    BOOKS 13–14   44
    BOOKS 15–16   47
    BOOKS 17–18   49
    BOOKS 19–20   52
    BOOKS 21–22   55
    BOOKS 23–24   58

IMPORTANT QUOTATIONS EXPLAINED   63

KEY FACTS   69

STUDY QUESTIONS   71

SUGGESTED ESSAY TOPICS   74

REVIEW & RESOURCES   75
    QUIZ   75
    SUGGESTIONS FOR FURTHER READING   80

Context

NEARLY THREE THOUSAND YEARS after they were composed, the *Iliad* and the *Odyssey* remain two of the most celebrated and widely read stories ever told, yet next to nothing is known about their composer. He was certainly an accomplished Greek bard, and he probably lived in the late eighth and early seventh centuries B.C. Authorship is traditionally ascribed to a blind poet named Homer, and it is under this name that the works are still published. Greeks of the third and second centuries B.C., however, already questioned whether Homer existed and whether the two epics were even written by a single individual.

Most modern scholars believe that even if a single person wrote the epics, his work owed a tremendous debt to a long tradition of unwritten, oral poetry. Stories of a glorious expedition to the East and of its leaders' fateful journeys home had been circulating in Greece for hundreds of years before the *Iliad* and *Odyssey* were composed. Casual storytellers and semiprofessional minstrels passed these stories down through generations, with each artist developing and polishing the story as he told it. According to this theory, one poet, multiple poets working in collaboration, or perhaps even a series of poets handing down their work in succession finally turned these stories into written works, again with each adding his own touch and expanding or contracting certain episodes in the overall narrative to fit his taste.

Although historical, archaeological, and linguistic evidence suggests that the epics were composed between 750 and 650 B.C. they are set in Mycenaean Greece in about the twelfth century B.C., during the Bronze Age. This earlier period, the Greeks believed, was a more glorious and sublime age, when gods still frequented the earth and heroic, godlike mortals with superhuman attributes populated Greece. Because the two epics strive to evoke this pristine age, they are written in a high style and generally depict life as it was believed to have been led in the great kingdoms of the Bronze Age. The Greeks are often referred to as "Achaeans," the name of a large tribe occupying Greece during the Bronze Age.

But Homer's reconstruction often yields to the realities of eighth- and seventh-century B.C. Greece. The feudal social structure apparent in the background of the *Odyssey* seems more akin to Homer's Greece than to Odysseus's, and Homer substitutes the pantheon of deities of his own day for the related but different gods whom Mycenaean Greeks worshipped. Many other minor but obvious anachronisms—such as references to iron tools and to tribes that had not yet migrated to Greece by the Bronze Age—betray the poem's later, Iron Age origins.

For centuries, many scholars believed that the Trojan War and its participants were entirely the creation of the Greek imagination. But in the late nineteenth century, an archaeologist named Heinrich Schliemann declared that he had discovered the remnants of Troy. The ruins that he uncovered sit a few dozen miles off of the Aegean coast in northwestern Turkey, a site that indeed fits the geographical descriptions of Homer's Troy. One layer of the site, roughly corresponding to the point in history when the fall of Troy would have taken place, shows evidence of fire and destruction consistent with a sack. Although most scholars accept Schliemann's discovered city as the site of the ancient city of Troy, many remain skeptical as to whether Homer's Trojan War ever really took place. Evidence from Near Eastern literature suggests that episodes similar to those described in the *Iliad* may have circulated even before Schliemann's Troy was destroyed. Nonetheless, many scholars now admit the possibility that some truth may lie at the center of the *Iliad,* hidden beneath many layers of poetic embellishment.

Like the *Odyssey,* the *Iliad* was composed primarily in the Ionic dialect of Ancient Greek, which was spoken on the Aegean islands and in the coastal settlements of Asia Minor, now modern Turkey. Some scholars thus conclude that the poet hailed from somewhere in the eastern Greek world. More likely, however, the poet chose the Ionic dialect because he felt it to be more appropriate for the high style and grand scope of his work. Slightly later Greek literature suggests that poets varied the dialects of their poems according to the themes that they were treating and might write in dialects that they didn't actually speak. Homer's epics are Panhellenic (encompassing all of Greece) in spirit and use forms from several other dialects. This suggests that Homer suited his poems to the dialect that would best complement his ideas.

The Aftermath of the Iliad

THE TROJAN WAR HAS NOT YET ENDED at the close of the *Iliad*. Homer's audience would have been familiar with the struggle's conclusion, and the potency of much of Homer's irony and foreboding depends on this familiarity. What follows is a synopsis of some of the most important events that happen after the *Iliad* ends.

THE DEATH OF ACHILLES

In the final books of the *Iliad*, Achilles refers frequently to his imminent death, about which his mother, Thetis, has warned him. After the end of the poem, at Hector's funeral feast, Achilles sights the beautiful Polyxena, the daughter of Priam and hence a princess of Troy. Taken with her beauty, Achilles falls in love with her. Hoping to marry her, he agrees to use his influence with the Achaean army to bring about an end to the war. But when he travels to the temple of Apollo to negotiate the peace, Paris shoots him in the heel—the only vulnerable part of his body—with a poisoned arrow. In other versions of the story, the wound occurs in the midst of battle.

ACHILLES' ARMOR AND THE DEATH OF AJAX

After Achilles' death, Ajax and Odysseus go and recover his body. Thetis instructs the Achaeans to bequeath Achilles' magnificent armor, forged by the god Hephaestus, to the most worthy hero. Both Ajax and Odysseus covet the armor; when it is awarded to Odysseus, Ajax commits suicide out of humiliation.

THE PALLADIUM AND THE ARROWS OF HERACLES

By the time of Achilles' and Ajax's deaths, Troy's defenses have been bolstered by the arrival of a new coalition of allies, including the Ethiopians and the Amazons. Achilles killed Penthesilea, the queen of the Amazons, before his death, but the Trojans continue to repel the Achaean assault. The gods relay to the Achaeans that they must perform a number of tasks in order to win the war: they must recover the arrows of Heracles, steal a statue of Athena called the Palladium from the temple in Troy, and perform various other challenges. Largely owing to the skill and courage of Odysseus and Diomedes, the Achaeans accomplish the tasks, and the Achaean archer Philoctetes later uses the arrows of Heracles to kill Paris. Despite this setback, Troy continues to hold against the Achaeans.

THE FALL OF TROY

The Achaean commanders are nearly ready to give up; nothing can penetrate the massive walls of Troy. But before they lose heart, Odysseus concocts a plan that will allow them to bypass the walls of the city completely. The Achaeans build a massive, hollow, wooden horse, large enough to hold a contingent of warriors inside. Odysseus and a group of soldiers hide in the horse, while the rest of the Achaeans burn their camps and sail away from Troy, waiting in their ships behind a nearby island.

The next morning, the Trojans peer down from the ramparts of their wall and discover the gigantic, mysterious horse. They also discover a lone Achaean soldier named Sinon, whom they take prisoner. As instructed by Odysseus, Sinon tells the Trojans that the Achaeans have incurred the wrath of Athena for the theft of the Palladium. They have left Sinon as a sacrifice to the goddess and constructed the horse as a gift to soothe her temper. Sinon explains that the Achaeans left the horse before the Trojan gates in the hopes that the Trojans would destroy it and thereby earn the wrath of Athena.

Believing Sinon's story, the Trojans wheel the massive horse into the city as a tribute to Athena. That night, Odysseus and his men slip out of the horse, kill the Trojan guards, and fling open the gates of Troy to the Achaean army, which has meanwhile approached the city again. Having at last penetrated the wall, the Achaeans massacre the citizens of Troy, plunder the city's riches, and burn the buildings to the ground. All of the Trojan men are killed except for a small group led by Aeneas, who escapes. Helen, whose loyalties have shifted back to the Achaeans since Paris's death, returns to Menelaus, and the Achaeans at last set sail for home.

AFTER THE WAR

The fates of many of the *Iliad*'s heroes after the war occupy an important space in Greek mythology. Odysseus, as foretold, spends ten years trying to return to Ithaca, and his adventures form the subject of Homer's other great epic, the *Odyssey*. Helen and Menelaus have a long and dangerous voyage back to their home in Sparta, with a long stay in Egypt. In the *Odyssey,* Telemachus travels to

Sparta in search of his father, Odysseus, and finds Helen and Mene-laus celebrating the marriage of their daughter, Hermione. Agamemnon, who has taken Priam's daughter Cassandra as a slave, returns home to his wife, Clytemnestra, and his kingdom, Mycenae. Ever since Agamemnon's sacrifice of Iphigeneia at the altar of Athena, however, Clytemnestra has nurtured a vast resentment toward her husband. She has taken a man named Aegisthus as her lover, and upon Agamemnon's return, the lovers murder Agamemnon in his bath and kill Cassandra as well. This story is the subject of Aeschylus's play *Agamemnon*. Meanwhile, Aeneas, the only great Trojan warrior to survive the fall of Troy, wanders for many years, searching for a new home for his surviving fellow citizens. His adventures are recounted in Virgil's epic *Aeneid*.

Plot Overview

N INE YEARS AFTER THE START OF THE TROJAN WAR, the Greek ("Achaean") army sacks Chryse, a town allied with Troy. During the battle, the Achaeans capture a pair of beautiful maidens, Chryseis and Briseis. Agamemnon, the leader of the Achaean forces, takes Chryseis as his prize, and Achilles, the Achaeans' greatest warrior, claims Briseis. Chryseis's father, Chryses, who serves as a priest of the god Apollo, offers an enormous ransom in return for his daughter, but Agamemnon refuses to give Chryseis back. Chryses then prays to Apollo, who sends a plague upon the Achaean camp.

After many Achaeans die, Agamemnon consults the prophet Calchas to determine the cause of the plague. When he learns that Chryseis is the cause, he reluctantly gives her up but then demands Briseis from Achilles as compensation. Furious at this insult, Achilles returns to his tent in the army camp and refuses to fight in the war any longer. He vengefully yearns to see the Achaeans destroyed and asks his mother, the sea-nymph Thetis, to enlist the services of Zeus, king of the gods, toward this end. The Trojan and Achaean sides have declared a cease-fire with each other, but now the Trojans breach the treaty and Zeus comes to their aid.

With Zeus supporting the Trojans and Achilles refusing to fight, the Achaeans suffer great losses. Several days of fierce conflict ensue, including duels between Paris and Menelaus and between Hector and Ajax. The Achaeans make no progress; even the heroism of the great Achaean warrior Diomedes proves fruitless. The Trojans push the Achaeans back, forcing them to take refuge behind the ramparts that protect their ships. The Achaeans begin to nurture some hope for the future when a nighttime reconnaissance mission by Diomedes and Odysseus yields information about the Trojans' plans, but the next day brings disaster. Several Achaean commanders become wounded, and the Trojans break through the Achaean ramparts. They advance all the way up to the boundary of the Achaean camp and set fire to one of the ships. Defeat seems imminent, because without the ships, the army will be stranded at Troy and almost certainly destroyed.

Concerned for his comrades but still too proud to help them himself, Achilles agrees to a plan proposed by Nestor that will allow his beloved friend Patroclus to take his place in battle, wearing his armor. Patroclus is a fine warrior, and his presence on the battlefield helps the Achaeans push the Trojans away from the ships and back to the city walls. But the counterattack soon falters. Apollo knocks Patroclus's armor to the ground, and Hector slays him. Fighting then breaks out as both sides try to lay claim to the body and armor. Hector ends up with the armor, but the Achaeans, thanks to a courageous effort by Menelaus and others, manage to bring the body back to their camp. When Achilles discovers that Hector has killed Patroclus, he fills with such grief and rage that he agrees to reconcile with Agamemnon and rejoin the battle. Thetis goes to Mount Olympus and persuades the god Hephaestus to forge Achilles a new suit of armor, which she presents to him the next morning. Achilles then rides out to battle at the head of the Achaean army.

Meanwhile, Hector, not expecting Achilles to rejoin the battle, has ordered his men to camp outside the walls of Troy. But when the Trojan army glimpses Achilles, it flees in terror back behind the city walls. Achilles cuts down every Trojan he sees. Strengthened by his rage, he even fights the god of the river Xanthus, who is angered that Achilles has caused so many corpses to fall into his streams. Finally, Achilles confronts Hector outside the walls of Troy. Ashamed at the poor advice that he gave his comrades, Hector refuses to flee inside the city with them. Achilles chases him around the city's periphery three times, but the goddess Athena finally tricks Hector into turning around and fighting Achilles. In a dramatic duel, Achilles kills Hector. He then lashes the body to the back of his chariot and drags it across the battlefield to the Achaean camp. Upon Achilles' arrival, the triumphant Achaeans celebrate Patroclus's funeral with a long series of athletic games in his honor. Each day for the next nine days, Achilles drags Hector's body in circles around Patroclus's funeral bier.

At last, the gods agree that Hector deserves a proper burial. Zeus sends the god Hermes to escort King Priam, Hector's father and the ruler of Troy, into the Achaean camp. Priam tearfully pleads with Achilles to take pity on a father bereft of his son and return Hector's body. He invokes the memory of Achilles' own father, Peleus. Deeply moved, Achilles finally relents and returns Hector's corpse to the Trojans. Both sides agree to a temporary truce, and Hector receives a hero's funeral.

Character List

The Achaeans (also called the "Argives" or "Danaans")

Achilles The son of the military man Peleus and the sea-nymph Thetis. The most powerful warrior in the *Iliad*, Achilles commands the Myrmidons, soldiers from his homeland of Phthia in Greece. Proud and headstrong, he takes offense easily and reacts with blistering indignation when he perceives that his honor has been slighted. Achilles' wrath at Agamemnon for taking his war prize, the maiden Briseis, forms the main subject of the *Iliad*.

Agamemnon (also called "Atrides") King of Mycenae and leader of the Achaean army; brother of King Menelaus of Sparta. Arrogant and often selfish, Agamemnon provides the Achaeans with strong but sometimes reckless and self-serving leadership. Like Achilles, he lacks consideration and forethought. Most saliently, his tactless appropriation of Achilles' war prize, the maiden Briseis, creates a crisis for the Achaeans, when Achilles, insulted, withdraws from the war.

Patroclus Achilles' beloved friend, companion, and advisor, Patroclus grew up alongside the great warrior in Phthia, under the guardianship of Peleus. Devoted to both Achilles and the Achaean cause, Patroclus stands by the enraged Achilles but also dons Achilles' terrifying armor in an attempt to hold the Trojans back.

Odysseus A fine warrior and the cleverest of the Achaean commanders. Along with Nestor, Odysseus is one of the Achaeans' two best public speakers. He helps mediate between Agamemnon and Achilles during their quarrel and often prevents them from making rash decisions.

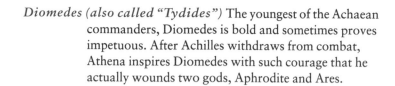

Diomedes (also called "Tydides") The youngest of the Achaean commanders, Diomedes is bold and sometimes proves impetuous. After Achilles withdraws from combat, Athena inspires Diomedes with such courage that he actually wounds two gods, Aphrodite and Ares.

Great Ajax An Achaean commander, Great Ajax (sometimes called "Telamonian Ajax" or simply "Ajax") is the second mightiest Achaean warrior after Achilles. His extraordinary size and strength help him to wound Hector twice by hitting him with boulders. He often fights alongside Little Ajax, and the pair is frequently referred to as the "Aeantes."

Little Ajax An Achaean commander, Little Ajax is the son of Oileus (to be distinguished from Great Ajax, the son of Telamon). He often fights alongside Great Ajax, whose stature and strength complement Little Ajax's small size and swift speed. The two together are sometimes called the "Aeantes."

Nestor King of Pylos and the oldest Achaean commander. Although age has taken much of Nestor's physical strength, it has left him with great wisdom. He often acts as an advisor to the military commanders, especially Agamemnon. Nestor and Odysseus are the Achaeans' most deft and persuasive orators, although Nestor's speeches are sometimes long-winded.

Menelaus King of Sparta; the younger brother of Agamemnon. While it is the abduction of his wife, Helen, by the Trojan prince Paris that sparks the Trojan War, Menelaus proves quieter, less imposing, and less arrogant than Agamemnon. Though he has a stout heart, Menelaus is not among the mightiest Achaean warriors.

Idomeneus King of Crete and a respected commander. Idomeneus leads a charge against the Trojans in Book 13.

Machaon A healer. Machaon is wounded by Paris in Book 11.

Calchas   An important soothsayer. Calchas's identification of the cause of the plague ravaging the Achaean army in Book 1 leads inadvertently to the rift between Agamemnon and Achilles that occupies the first nineteen books of the *Iliad*.

Peleus   Achilles' father and the grandson of Zeus. Although his name often appears in the epic, Peleus never appears in person. Priam powerfully invokes the memory of Peleus when he convinces Achilles to return Hector's corpse to the Trojans in Book 24.

Phoenix   A kindly old warrior, Phoenix helped raise Achilles while he himself was still a young man. Achilles deeply loves and trusts Phoenix, and Phoenix mediates between him and Agamemnon during their quarrel.

The Myrmidons   The soldiers under Achilles' command, hailing from Achilles' homeland, Phthia.

THE TROJANS

Hector   A son of King Priam and Queen Hecuba, Hector is the mightiest warrior in the Trojan army. He mirrors Achilles in some of his flaws, but his bloodlust is not so great as that of Achilles. He is devoted to his wife, Andromache, and son, Astyanax, but resents his brother Paris for bringing war upon their family and city.

Priam   King of Troy and husband of Hecuba, Priam is the father of fifty Trojan warriors, including Hector and Paris. Though too old to fight, he has earned the respect of both the Trojans and the Achaeans by virtue of his level-headed, wise, and benevolent rule. He treats Helen kindly, though he laments the war that her beauty has sparked.

Hecuba   Queen of Troy, wife of Priam, and mother of Hector and Paris.

Paris (also known as "Alexander") A son of Priam and Hecuba and brother of Hector. Paris's abduction of the beautiful Helen, wife of Menelaus, sparked the Trojan War. Paris is self-centered and often unmanly. He fights effectively with a bow and arrow (never with the more manly sword or spear) but often lacks the spirit for battle and prefers to sit in his room making love to Helen while others fight for him, thus earning both Hector's and Helen's scorn.

Helen Reputed to be the most beautiful woman in the ancient world, Helen left her husband, Menelaus, to run away with Paris. She loathes herself now for the misery that she has caused so many Trojan and Achaean men. Although her contempt extends to Paris as well, she continues to stay with him.

Aeneas A Trojan nobleman, the son of Aphrodite, and a mighty warrior. The Romans believed that Aeneas later founded their city (he is the protagonist of Virgil's masterpiece the *Aeneid*).

Andromache Hector's loving wife, Andromache begs Hector to withdraw from the war and save himself before the Achaeans kill him.

Astyanax Hector and Andromache's infant son.

Polydamas A young Trojan commander, Polydamas sometimes figures as a foil for Hector, proving cool-headed and prudent when Hector charges ahead. Polydamas gives the Trojans sound advice, but Hector seldom acts on it.

Glaucus A powerful Trojan warrior, Glaucus nearly fights a duel with Diomedes. The men's exchange of armor after they realize that their families are friends illustrates the value that ancients placed on kinship and camaraderie.

Agenor A Trojan warrior who attempts to fight Achilles in Book 21. Agenor delays Achilles long enough for the Trojan army to flee inside Troy's walls.

Dolon   A Trojan sent to spy on the Achaean camp in Book 10.

Pandarus A Trojan archer. Pandarus's shot at Menelaus in Book 4 breaks the temporary truce between the two sides.

Antenor   A Trojan nobleman, advisor to King Priam, and father of many Trojan warriors. Antenor argues that Helen should be returned to Menelaus in order to end the war, but Paris refuses to give her up.

Sarpedon One of Zeus's sons. Sarpedon's fate seems intertwined with the gods' quibbles, calling attention to the unclear nature of the gods' relationship to Fate.

Chryseis Chryses's daughter, a priest of Apollo in a Trojan-allied town.

Briseis   A war prize of Achilles. When Agamemnon is forced to return Chryseis to her father, he appropriates Briseis as compensation, sparking Achilles' great rage.

Chryses   A priest of Apollo in a Trojan-allied town; the father of Chryseis, whom Agamemnon takes as a war prize.

THE GODS AND IMMORTALS

Zeus   King of the gods and husband of Hera, Zeus claims neutrality in the mortals' conflict and often tries to keep the other gods from participating in it. However, he throws his weight behind the Trojan side for much of the battle after the sulking Achilles has his mother, Thetis, ask the god to do so.

Hera   Queen of the gods and Zeus's wife, Hera is a conniving, headstrong woman. She often goes behind Zeus's back in matters on which they disagree, working with Athena to crush the Trojans, whom she passionately hates.

Athena The goddess of wisdom, purposeful battle, and the womanly arts; Zeus's daughter. Like Hera, Athena passionately hates the Trojans and often gives the Achaeans valuable aid.

Thetis A sea-nymph and the devoted mother of Achilles, Thetis gets Zeus to help the Trojans and punish the Achaeans at the request of her angry son. When Achilles finally rejoins the battle, she commissions Hephaestus to design him a new suit of armor.

Apollo A son of Zeus and twin brother of the goddess Artemis, Apollo is god of the arts and archery. He supports the Trojans and often intervenes in the war on their behalf.

Aphrodite Goddess of love and daughter of Zeus, Aphrodite is married to Hephaestus but maintains a romantic relationship with Ares. She supports Paris and the Trojans throughout the war, though she proves somewhat ineffectual in battle.

Poseidon The brother of Zeus and god of the sea. Poseidon holds a long-standing grudge against the Trojans because they never paid him for helping them to build their city. He therefore supports the Achaeans in the war.

Hephaestus God of fire and husband of Aphrodite, Hephaestus is the gods' metalsmith and is known as the lame or crippled god. Although the text doesn't make clear his sympathies in the mortals' struggle, he helps the Achaeans by forging a new set of armor for Achilles and by rescuing Achilles during his fight with a river god.

Artemis Goddess of the hunt, daughter of Zeus, and twin sister of Apollo. Artemis supports the Trojans in the war.

Ares God of war and lover of Aphrodite, Ares generally supports the Trojans in the war.

Hermes The messenger of the gods. Hermes escorts Priam to Achilles' tent in Book 24.

Iris Zeus's messenger.

ANALYSIS OF MAJOR CHARACTERS

ACHILLES

Although Achilles possesses superhuman strength and has a close relationship with the gods, he may strike modern readers as less than heroic. He has all the marks of a great warrior, and indeed proves the mightiest man in the Achaean army, but his deep-seated character flaws constantly impede his ability to act with nobility and integrity. He cannot control his pride or the rage that surges up when that pride is injured. This attribute so poisons him that he abandons his comrades and even prays that the Trojans will slaughter them, all because he has been slighted at the hands of his commander, Agamemnon. Achilles is driven primarily by a thirst for glory. Part of him yearns to live a long, easy life, but he knows that his personal fate forces him to choose between the two. Ultimately, he is willing to sacrifice everything else so that his name will be remembered.

Like most Homeric characters, Achilles does not develop significantly over the course of the epic. Although the death of Patroclus prompts him to seek reconciliation with Agamemnon, it does not alleviate his rage, but instead redirects it toward Hector. The event does not make Achilles a more deliberative or self-reflective character. Bloodlust, wrath, and pride continue to consume him. He mercilessly mauls his opponents, brazenly takes on the river Xanthus, ignobly desecrates the body of Hector, and savagely sacrifices twelve Trojan men at the funeral of Patroclus. He does not relent in this brutality until the final book of the epic, when King Priam, begging for the return of Hector's desecrated corpse, appeals to Achilles' memory of his father, Peleus. Yet it remains unclear whether a father's heartbroken pleas really have transformed Achilles, or whether this scene merely testifies to Achilles' capacity for grief and acquaintance with anguish, which were already proven in his intense mourning of Patroclus.

AGAMEMNON

Agamemnon, king of Mycenae and commander-in-chief of the Achaean army, resembles Achilles in some respects. Though not nearly as strong, he has a similarly hot temper and prideful streak. When Agamemnon's insulting demand that Achilles relinquish his war prize, Briseis, causes Achilles to withdraw angrily from battle, the suffering that results for the Greek army owes as much to Agamemnon's stubbornness as to that of Achilles. But Agamemnon's pride makes him more arrogant than Achilles. While Achilles' pride flares up after it is injured, Agamemnon uses every opportunity to make others feel the effects of his. He always expects the largest portions of the plunder, even though he takes the fewest risks in battle. Additionally, he insists upon leading the army, even though his younger brother Menelaus, whose wife, Helen, was stolen by Paris, possesses the real grievance against the Trojans. He never allows the Achaeans to forget his kingly status.

Agamemnon also differs from Achilles in his appreciation of subtlety. Achilles remains fiercely devoted to those who love him but devotedly vicious to those who do him harm; he sees no shades of gray. Agamemnon, however, remains fundamentally concerned with himself, and he has the cunning to manipulate people and situations for his own benefit. He does not trust his troops blindly, but tests their loyalty, as in Book 2. Although he reconciles with Achilles in Book 19, he shirks personal responsibility with a forked-tongued indictment of Fate, Ruin, and the gods. Whereas Achilles is wholly consumed by his emotions, Agamemnon demonstrates a deft ability to keep himself—and others—under control. When he commits wrongs, he does so not out of blind rage and frustration like Achilles, but out of amoral, self-serving cunning. For this reason, Homer's portrait of Agamemnon ultimately proves unkind, and the reader never feels the same sympathy for him as for Achilles.

HECTOR

Hector is the mightiest warrior in the Trojan army. Although he meets his match in Achilles, he wreaks havoc on the Achaean army during Achilles' period of absence. He leads the assault that finally penetrates the Achaean ramparts, he is the first and only Trojan to set fire to an Achaean ship, and he kills Patroclus. Yet his leadership contains discernible flaws, especially toward the end of the epic, when the participation of first Patroclus and then Achilles reinvigorates the Achaean army. He demonstrates a certain cowardice when, twice in Book 17, he flees Great Ajax. Indeed, he recovers his courage only after receiving the insults of his comrades—first Glaucus and then Aeneas. He can often become emotionally carried away as well, treating Patroclus and his other victims with rash cruelty. Later, swept up by a burst of confidence, he foolishly orders the Trojans to camp outside Troy's walls the night before Achilles returns to battle, thus causing a crucial downfall the next day.

But although Hector may prove overly impulsive and insufficiently prudent, he does not come across as arrogant or overbearing, as Agamemnon does. Moreover, the fact that Hector fights in his homeland, unlike any of the Achaean commanders, allows Homer to develop him as a tender, family-oriented man. Hector shows deep, sincere love for his wife and children. Indeed, he even treats his brother Paris with forgiveness and indulgence, despite the man's lack of spirit and preference for lovemaking over military duty. Hector never turns violent with him, merely aiming frustrated words at his cowardly brother. Moreover, although Hector loves his family, he never loses sight of his responsibility to Troy. Admittedly, he runs from Achilles at first and briefly entertains the delusional hope of negotiating his way out of a duel. However, in the end he stands up to the mighty warrior, even when he realizes that the gods have abandoned him. His refusal to flee even in the face of vastly superior forces makes him the most tragic figure in the poem.

THEMES, MOTIFS & SYMBOLS

THEMES

Themes are the fundamental and often universal ideas explored in a literary work.

THE GLORY OF WAR

One can make a strong argument that the *Iliad* seems to celebrate war. Characters emerge as worthy or despicable based on their degree of competence and bravery in battle. Paris, for example, doesn't like to fight, and correspondingly receives the scorn of both his family and his lover. Achilles, on the other hand, wins eternal glory by explicitly rejecting the option of a long, comfortable, uneventful life at home. The text itself seems to support this means of judging character and extends it even to the gods. The epic holds up warlike deities such as Athena for the reader's admiration while it makes fun of gods who run from aggression, using the timidity of Aphrodite and Artemis to create a scene of comic relief. To fight is to prove one's honor and integrity, while to avoid warfare is to demonstrate laziness, ignoble fear, or misaligned priorities.

To be sure, the *Iliad* doesn't ignore the realities of war. Men die gruesome deaths; women become slaves and concubines, estranged from their tearful fathers and mothers; a plague breaks out in the Achaean camp and decimates the army. In the face of these horrors, even the mightiest warriors occasionally experience fear, and the poet tells us that both armies regret that the war ever began. Though Achilles points out that all men, whether brave or cowardly, meet the same death in the end, the poem never asks the reader to question the legitimacy of the ongoing struggle. Homer never implies that the fight constitutes a waste of time or human life. Rather, he portrays each side as having a justifiable reason to fight and depicts warfare as a respectable and even glorious manner of settling the dispute.

MILITARY GLORY OVER FAMILY LIFE

A theme in the *Iliad* closely related to the glory of war is the predominance of military glory over family. The text clearly admires the reciprocal bonds of deference and obligation that bind Homeric families together, but it respects much more highly the pursuit of *kleos,* the "glory" or "renown" that one wins in the eyes of others by performing great deeds. Homer constantly forces his characters to choose between their loved ones and the quest for kleos, and the most heroic characters invariably choose the latter. Andromache pleads with Hector not to risk orphaning his son, but Hector knows that fighting among the front ranks represents the only means of "winning my father great glory." Paris, on the other hand, chooses to spend time with Helen rather than fight in the war; accordingly, both the text and the other characters treat him with derision. Achilles debates returning home to live in ease with his aging father, but he remains at Troy to win glory by killing Hector and avenging Patroclus. The gravity of the decisions that Hector and Achilles make is emphasized by the fact that each knows his fate ahead of time. The characters prize so highly the martial values of honor, noble bravery, and glory that they willingly sacrifice the chance to live a long life with those they love.

THE IMPERMANENCE OF HUMAN LIFE AND ITS CREATIONS

Although the *Iliad* chronicles a very brief period in a very long war, it remains acutely conscious of the specific ends awaiting each of the people involved. Troy is destined to fall, as Hector explains to his wife in Book 6. The text announces that Priam and all of his children will die—Hector dies even before the close of the poem. Achilles will meet an early end as well, although not within the pages of the *Iliad.* Homer constantly alludes to this event, especially toward the end of the epic, making clear that even the greatest of men cannot escape death. Indeed, he suggests that the very greatest—the noblest and bravest—may yield to death sooner than others.

Similarly, the *Iliad* recognizes, and repeatedly reminds its readers, that the creations of mortals have a mortality of their own. The glory of men does not live on in their constructions, institutions, or cities. The prophecy of Calchas, as well as Hector's tender words with Andromache and the debates of the gods, constantly remind the reader that Troy's lofty ramparts will fall. But the Greek fortifications will not last much longer. Though the Greeks erect their bulwarks only partway into the epic, Apollo and Poseidon plan their destruction as early as Book 12. The poem thus emphasizes the ephemeral nature of human beings and their world, suggesting that mortals should try to live their lives as honorably as possible, so that they will be remembered well. For if mortals' physical bodies and material creations cannot survive them, perhaps their words and deeds can. Certainly the existence of Homer's poem would attest to this notion.

MOTIFS

Motifs are recurring structures, contrasts, or literary devices that can help to develop and inform the text's major themes.

ARMOR

One would naturally expect a martial epic to depict men in arms, but armor in the *Iliad* emerges as something more than merely a protective cover for a soldier's body. In fact, Homer often portrays a hero's armor as having an aura of its own, separate from its wearer. In one of the epic's more tender scenes, Hector removes his helmet to keep its horsehair crest from frightening his son Astyanax. When Patroclus wears Achilles' armor to scare the Trojans and drive them from the ships, Apollo and Hector quickly see through the disguise. Then, when a fight breaks out over Patroclus's fallen body, the armor goes one way and the corpse another. Hector dons the armor, but it ends up betraying him, as it were, in favor of its former owner. Achilles' knowledge of its vulnerabilities makes it easier for him to run Hector through with his sword. By this point in the story, Achilles has a new set of armor, fashioned by the god Hephaestus, which also seems to have a life of its own. While Achilles' mortal body can be wounded—and indeed, the poem reminds us of Achilles' impending death on many occasions—Homer describes the divine armor as virtually impervious to assault.

BURIAL

While martial epics naturally touch upon the subject of burial, the *Iliad* lingers over it. The burial of Hector is given particular attention, as it marks the melting of Achilles' crucial rage. The mighty Trojan receives a spectacular funeral that comes only after an equally spectacular fight over his corpse. Patroclus's burial also receives much attention in the text, as Homer devotes an entire book to the funeral and games in the warrior's honor. The poem also describes burials unconnected to particular characters, such as in Book 7, when both armies undertake a large-scale burial of their largely unnamed dead. The *Iliad*'s interest in burial partly reflects the interests of ancient Greek culture as a whole, which stressed proper burial as a requirement for the soul's peaceful rest. However, it also reflects the grim outlook of the *Iliad*, its interest in the relentlessness of fate and the impermanence of human life.

Fire

Fire emerges as a recurrent image in the *Iliad*, often associated with internal passions such as fury or rage, but also with their external manifestations. Homer describes Achilles as "blazing" in Book 1 and compares the sparkle of his freshly donned armor to the sun. Moreover, the poem often compares a hero's charge or an onslaught of troops to a conflagration sweeping through a field. But fire doesn't appear just allegorically or metaphorically; it appears materially as well. The Trojans light fires in Book 8 to watch the Achaean army and to prevent it from slipping away by night. They constantly threaten the Achaean ships with fire and indeed succeed in torching one of them. Thus, whether present literally or metaphorically, the frequency with which fire appears in the *Iliad* indicates the poem's overarching concern with instances of profound power and destruction.

Symbols

Symbols are objects, characters, figures, or colors used to represent abstract ideas or concepts.

The Achaean Ships

The Achaean ships symbolize the future of the Greek race. They constitute the army's only means of conveying itself home, whether in triumph or defeat. Even if the Achaean army were to lose the war, the ships could bring back survivors; the ships' destruction, however, would mean the annihilation—or automatic exile—of every last soldier. Homer implies that some men shirked the war and stayed in Greece, while others, such as Peleus, were too old to fight. However, to Homer's original audience, the Achaean warriors at Troy represented more than a mere subpopulation of the Greek race. Homer's contemporaries believed that the heroes represented here actually lived historically, as real kings who ruled the various city-states of Greece in their earliest years. Ancient audiences regarded them as playing definitive roles in the formation and development of Greece as they knew it. The mass death of these leaders and role models would have meant the decimation of a civilization.

THE SHIELD OF ACHILLES

The *Iliad* is an extremely compressed narrative. Although it treats many of the themes of human experience, it does so within the scope of a few days out of a ten-year war. The shield constitutes only a tiny part in this martial saga, a single piece of armor on a single man in one of the armies—yet it provides perspective on the entire war. Depicting normal life in peacetime, it symbolizes the world beyond the battlefield, and implies that war constitutes only one aspect of existence. Life as a whole, the shield reminds us, includes feasts and dances and marketplaces and crops being harvested. Human beings may serve not only as warriors but also as artisans and laborers in the fields. Not only do they work, they also play, as the shield depicts with its dancing children. Interestingly, although Homer glorifies war and the life of the warrior throughout most of his epic, his depiction of everyday life as it appears on the shield comes across as equally noble, perhaps preferable.

SYMBOLS

Summary & Analysis

Book 1

Rage—Goddess, sing the rage of Peleus' son Achilles,
murderous, doomed, that cost the Achaeans countless losses
                        (See QUOTATIONS, p. 63)

SUMMARY

The poet invokes a muse to aid him in telling the story of the rage of Achilles, the greatest Greek hero to fight in the Trojan War. The narrative begins nine years after the start of the war, as the Achaeans sack a Trojan-allied town and capture two beautiful maidens, Chryseis and Briseis. Agamemnon, commander-in-chief of the Achaean army, takes Chryseis as his prize. Achilles, one of the Achaeans' most valuable warriors, claims Briseis. Chryseis's father, a man named Chryses who serves as a priest of the god Apollo, begs Agamemnon to return his daughter and offers to pay an enormous ransom. When Agamemnon refuses, Chryses prays to Apollo for help.

Apollo sends a plague upon the Greek camp, causing the death of many soldiers. After ten days of suffering, Achilles calls an assembly of the Achaean army and asks for a soothsayer to reveal the cause of the plague. Calchas, a powerful seer, stands up and offers his services. Though he fears retribution from Agamemnon, Calchas reveals the plague as a vengeful and strategic move by Chryses and Apollo. Agamemnon flies into a rage and says that he will return Chryseis only if Achilles gives him Briseis as compensation.

Agamemnon's demand humiliates and infuriates the proud Achilles. The men argue, and Achilles threatens to withdraw from battle and take his people, the Myrmidons, back home to Phthia. Agamemnon threatens to go to Achilles' tent in the army's camp and take Briseis himself. Achilles stands poised to draw his sword and kill the Achaean commander when the goddess Athena, sent by Hera, the queen of the gods, appears to him and checks his anger. Athena's guidance, along with a speech by the wise advisor Nestor, finally succeeds in preventing the duel.

That night, Agamemnon puts Chryseis on a ship back to her father and sends heralds to have Briseis escorted from Achilles' tent.

Achilles prays to his mother, the sea-nymph Thetis, to ask Zeus, king of the gods, to punish the Achaeans. He relates to her the tale of his quarrel with Agamemnon, and she promises to take the matter up with Zeus—who owes her a favor—as soon as he returns from a thirteen-day period of feasting with the Aethiopians. Meanwhile, the Achaean commander Odysseus is navigating the ship that Chryseis has boarded. When he lands, he returns the maiden and makes sacrifices to Apollo. Chryses, overjoyed to see his daughter, prays to the god to lift the plague from the Achaean camp. Apollo acknowledges his prayer, and Odysseus returns to his comrades.

But the end of the plague on the Achaeans only marks the beginning of worse suffering. Ever since his quarrel with Agamemnon, Achilles has refused to participate in battle, and, after twelve days, Thetis makes her appeal to Zeus, as promised. Zeus is reluctant to help the Trojans, for his wife, Hera, favors the Greeks, but he finally agrees. Hera becomes livid when she discovers that Zeus is helping the Trojans, but her son Hephaestus persuades her not to plunge the gods into conflict over the mortals.

———————————

ANALYSIS

Like other ancient epic poems, the *Iliad* presents its subject clearly from the outset. Indeed, the poem names its focus in its opening word: menin, or "rage." Specifically, the *Iliad* concerns itself with the rage of Achilles—how it begins, how it cripples the Achaean army, and how it finally becomes redirected toward the Trojans. Although the Trojan War as a whole figures prominently in the work, this larger conflict ultimately provides the text with background rather than subject matter. By the time Achilles and Agamemnon enter their quarrel, the Trojan War has been going on for nearly ten years. Achilles' absence from battle, on the other hand, lasts only a matter of days, and the epic ends soon after his return. The poem describes neither the origins nor the end of the war that frames Achilles' wrath. Instead, it scrutinizes the origins and the end of this wrath, thus narrowing the scope of the poem from a larger conflict between warring peoples to a smaller one between warring individuals.

But while the poem focuses most centrally on the rage of a mortal, it also concerns itself greatly with the motivations and actions of the gods. Even before Homer describes the quarrel between Achilles and Agamemnon, he explains that Apollo was responsible for the conflict. In general, the gods in the poem participate in mortal affairs in two ways. First, they act as external forces upon the course of events, as when Apollo sends the plague upon the Achaean army. Second, they represent internal forces acting on individuals, as when Athena, the goddess of wisdom, prevents Achilles from abandoning all reason and persuades him to cut Agamemnon with words and insults rather than his sword. But while the gods serve a serious function in partially determining grave matters of peace and violence, life and death, they also serve one final function—that of comic relief. Their intrigues, double-dealings, and inane squabbles often appear humorously petty in comparison with the wholesale slaughter that pervades the mortal realm. The bickering between Zeus and Hera, for example, provides a much lighter parallel to the heated exchange between Agamemnon and Achilles.

Indeed, in their submission to base appetites and shallow grudges, the gods of the *Iliad* often seem more prone to human folly than the human characters themselves. Zeus promises to help the Trojans not out of any profound moral consideration but rather because he owes Thetis a favor. Similarly, his hesitation in making this promise stems not from some worthy desire to let fate play itself out but from his fear of annoying his wife. When Hera does indeed become annoyed, Zeus is able to silence her only by threatening to strangle her. Such instances of partisanship, hurt feelings, and domestic strife, common among the gods of the *Iliad*, portray the gods and goddesses as less invincible and imperturbable than we might imagine them to be. We expect these sorts of excessive sensitivities and occasionally dysfunctional relationships of the human characters but not the divine ones.

The clash between Achilles and Agamemnon highlights one of the most dominant aspects of the ancient Greek value system: the vital importance of personal honor. Both Agamemnon and Achilles prioritize their respective individual glories over the well-being of the Achaean forces. Agamemnon believes that, as chief of the Achaean forces, he deserves the highest available prize—Briseis— and is thus willing to antagonize Achilles, the most crucial Achaean warrior, to secure what he believes is properly owed to him. Achilles would rather defend his claim to Briseis, his personal spoil of victory and thus what he believes is properly owed to him, than defuse the situation. Each man considers deferring to the other a humiliation rather than an act of honor or duty; each thus puts his own interest ahead of that of his people, jeopardizing the war effort.

BOOK 2

SUMMARY

To help the Trojans, as promised, Zeus sends a false dream to Agamemnon in which a figure in the form of Nestor persuades Agamemnon that he can take Troy if he launches a full-scale assault on the city's walls. The next day, Agamemnon gathers his troops for attack, but, to test their courage, he lies and tells them that he has decided to give up the war and return to Greece. To his dismay, they eagerly run to their ships.

When Hera sees the Achaeans fleeing, she alerts Athena, who inspires Odysseus, the most eloquent of the Achaeans, to call the men back. He shouts words of encouragement and insult to goad their pride and restore their confidence. He reminds them of the prophecy that the soothsayer Calchas gave when the Achaeans were first mustering their soldiers back in Greece: a water snake had slithered to shore and devoured a nest of nine sparrows, and Calchas interpreted the sign to mean that nine years would pass before the Achaeans would finally take Troy. As Odysseus reminds them, they vowed at that time that they would not abandon their struggle until the city fell.

Nestor now encourages Agamemnon to arrange his troops by city and clan so that they can fight side by side with their friends and kin. The poet takes this opportunity to enter into a catalog of the army. After invoking the muses to aid his memory, he details the cities that have contributed troops to the Greek cause, the number of troops that each has contributed, and who leads each contingent. At the end of the list, the poet singles out the bravest of the Achaeans, Achilles and Ajax among them. When Zeus sends a messenger to the Trojan court, telling them of the Greeks' awesome formation, the Trojans muster their own troops under the command of Priam's son Hector. The poet then catalogs the Trojan forces.

ANALYSIS

By the end of Book 2, Homer has introduced all of the *Iliad*'s major characters on the Greek side—his catalog of the Trojan troops at the end of Book 2 leads naturally into an introduction of the Trojan leadership in Book 3. The poem has already established the characters of Agamemnon, proud and headstrong, and Achilles, mighty but temperamental, whose quarrel dominates the epic. Now the poet provides description of two supporting actors, Odysseus and Nestor. Though both of these figures appear in Book 1, the army's flight to its ships in Book 2 motivates their first important speeches and thus establishes a crucial component of their role in the epic: they are the wise, foresighted advisors whose shrewdness and clarity of mind will keep the Achaeans on their course. Furthermore, in successfully restoring the troops' morale, Odysseus and Nestor confirm their reputation as the Achaeans' most talented rhetoricians.

In addition to prompting the speeches of Odysseus and Nestor, the Achaeans' flight to the ships serves three other important purposes in the narrative. First, it shows just how dire the Greek situation has become: even the army's foremost leader, Agamemnon, has failed to recognize the low morale of the troops; he is wholly blindsided by his men's willingness to give up the war. The eagerness with which the troops flee back to the harbor not only testifies to the suffering that they must have already endured but also bodes ill for their future efforts, which will prove much harder given the soldiers' homesickness and lack of motivation. But second, and on the other hand, by pointing out the intensity of the Greeks' suffering, the episode emphasizes the glory of the Greeks' eventual victory. Homer's audience knew well that the war between the Greeks and Trojans ended in Troy's defeat. This episode indicates just how close the Greek army came to abandoning the effort entirely and returning to Greece in disgrace. That the troops prove able to rise from the depths of despair to the heights of military triumph conveys the immensity of the Greek achievement.

Third, the flight to the ships indirectly results in the famous catalog of the Achaean forces. Nestor's advice that the troops be arranged by city ensures that the soldiers will be motivated: by fighting side by side with their closest friends, they will have an emotional investment in the army's success, and their leaders will more easily be able to identify them as either cowardly or courageous. While the catalog of forces may seem rather tedious to modern readers—though it does build tension by setting up an all-out conflict—it would have greatly inspired Homeric audiences. Even the effort seemingly necessary to recount the catalog is epic and grandiose. The poet seems to invoke all nine Muses as he proclaims, "The mass of troops I could never tally . . . / not even if I had ten tongues and ten mouths" (2.577–578). The sack of Troy was a Panhellenic effort, and even the smallest cities played a part. Each Greek who heard the tale could take pride in hearing the name of his city and its ancient, mythic leaders mentioned as participants in this heroic achievement. By calling these men to mind, Homer doesn't bore his audience but rather stirs them, evoking their honorable heritage.

BOOKS 3–4

SUMMARY: BOOK 3

The Trojan army marches from the city gates and advances to meet the Achaeans. Paris, the Trojan prince who precipitated the war by stealing the beautiful Helen from her husband, Menelaus, challenges the Achaeans to single combat with any of their warriors. When Menelaus steps forward, however, Paris loses heart and shrinks back into the Trojan ranks. Hector, Paris's brother and the leader of the Trojan forces, chastises Paris for his cowardice. Stung by Hector's insult, Paris finally agrees to a duel with Menelaus, declaring that the contest will establish peace between Trojans and Achaeans by deciding once and for all which man shall have Helen as his wife. Hector presents the terms to Menelaus, who accepts. Both armies look forward to ending the war at last.

As Paris and Menelaus prepare for combat, the goddess Iris, disguised as Hector's sister Laodice, visits Helen in Priam's palace. Iris urges Helen to go to the city gates and witness the battle about to be fought over her. Helen finds the city's elders, including Priam, gathered there. Priam asks Helen about the strapping young Achaeans he sees, and she identifies Agamemnon, Ajax, and Odysseus. Priam marvels at their strength and splendor but eventually leaves the scene, unable to bear watching Paris fight to the death.

Paris and Menelaus arm themselves and begin their duel. Neither is able to fell the other with his spear. Menelaus breaks his sword over Paris's helmet. He then grabs Paris by the helmet and begins dragging him through the dirt, but Aphrodite, an ally of the Trojans, snaps the strap of the helmet so that it breaks off in Menelaus's hands. Frustrated, Menelaus retrieves his spear and is about to drive it home into Paris when Aphrodite whisks Paris away to his room in Priam's palace. She summons Helen there too. Helen, after upbraiding Paris for his cowardice, lies down in bed with him. Back on the battlefield, both the Trojans and the Greeks search for Paris, who seems to have magically disappeared. Agamemnon insists that Menelaus has won the duel, and he demands Helen back.

SUMMARY: BOOK 4

Meanwhile, the gods engage in their own duels. Zeus argues that Menelaus has lost the duel and that the war should end as the mortals had agreed. But Hera, who has invested much in the Achaean cause, wants nothing less than the complete destruction of Troy. In the end, Zeus gives way and sends Athena to the battlefield to rekindle the fighting. Disguised as a Trojan soldier, Athena convinces the archer Pandarus to take aim at Menelaus. Pandarus fires, but Athena, who wants merely to give the Achaeans a pretext for fighting, deflects the arrow so that it only wounds Menelaus.

Agamemnon now rallies the Achaean ranks. He meets Nestor, Odysseus, and Diomedes, among others, and spurs them on by challenging their pride or recounting the great deeds of their fathers. Battle breaks out, and the blood flows freely. None of the major characters is killed or wounded, but Odysseus and Great Ajax kill a number of minor Trojan figures. The gods also become involved, with Athena helping the Achaeans and Apollo helping the Trojans. The efforts toward a truce have failed utterly.

ANALYSIS: BOOKS 3–4

While the first two books introduce the commanders of the Achaean forces, the next two introduce the Trojan forces. Priam, Hector, Paris, and Helen of Troy (formerly, of course, queen of Sparta) all make their first appearances in Book 3, and their personalities begin to emerge. In particular, Paris's glibness throws him into stark contrast with Hector and many of the Achaean leaders whom the audience has already encountered. While the sight of Menelaus causes Paris to flee, Hector, much more devoted to the ideal of heroic honor, criticizes him for the disgrace that he has brought upon not only himself but also the entire Trojan army. Paris's fight with Menelaus proves embarrassing, and he must be rescued—not by any particularly fierce deity but rather by Aphrodite, the goddess of love (she is even referred to, in Book 5, as the "coward goddess" [5.371]). Though Paris sulkily blames his misfortune in the fight on the gods whom he claims aided Menelaus, Homer himself makes no mention of these gods, and the suffering that Menelaus undergoes in the fight suggests that he had no divine help. But perhaps most outrageous is Paris's retreat to his marriage bed. While the rest of the Trojan army is forced to fight for the woman whom he stole from the Achaeans, he sleeps with her. This affront to the heroic code of conduct disgusts even the Trojan rank and file, who, we read, "hated [Paris] like death" (3.533).

The other Trojan characters emerge much more sympathetically, and the poem presents its first mortal female character, Helen, in a warm light. Although Helen ran away with Paris and thus bears some of the responsibility for the deaths of so many of her country-men, unlike Paris, she doesn't take her role in the carnage lightly. Her labeling of herself a "hateful" creature and her admission that she wishes that she had died the day Paris brought her to Troy dem-onstrate her shame and self-loathing (3.467). Her remorseful reflec-tions upon the homeland that she left behind as she surveys the Achaean ranks arrayed beneath the walls of Troy further reveal her regret and sense of having done wrong. The scene becomes particu-larly poignant when she wonders whether her brothers Castor and Polydeuces, whom she cannot find in the crowd, might possibly have refused to join the Greek expedition and fight for such an accursed sister. Tragically, she doesn't realize, as Homer points out, that their absence signifies not their anger but their death in battle.

The *Iliad* presents no clear villains. Though the story is told from the Greek perspective, it doesn't demonize the Trojans. In fact, in wars that occurred before the start of the poem, such as the struggle against the Amazons that Priam mentions, the Trojans allied with the Achaeans. Both armies suffer in the current violence, and both feel relieved to hear that the duel between Menelaus and Paris may end it. When the two sides consecrate their truce with a sacrifice, sol-diers in both armies pray that, should the cease-fire be broken, the guilty side be butchered and its women raped—whichever side that may be. When the cease-fire does fail and open conflict between the two armies erupts for the first time in the epic, the carnage consumes both sides with equally horrific intensity. Furthermore, the text doesn't unequivocally imply the Trojans' guilt in the breach—Pan-darus shoots at Menelaus only under Athena's persuasion. Indeed, the gods seem to be the only ones who take pleasure in the conflict, and the mortals, like toy soldiers, provide Hera and Athena an easy way to settle their disagreement with Zeus.

BOOKS 5-6

SUMMARY: BOOK 5

> *Ah what chilling blows*
> *we suffer—thanks to our own conflicting wills—*
> *whenever we show these mortal men some kindness.*
> (See QUOTATIONS, p. 64)

As the battle rages, Pandarus wounds the Achaean hero Diomedes. Diomedes prays to Athena for revenge, and the goddess endows him with superhuman strength and the extraordinary power to discern gods on the field of battle. She warns him, however, not to challenge any of them except Aphrodite. Diomedes fights like a man possessed, slaughtering all Trojans he meets. The overconfident Pandarus meets a gruesome death at the end of Diomedes' spear, and Aeneas, the noble Trojan hero immortalized in Virgil's *Aeneid*, likewise receives a wounding at the hands of the divinely assisted Diomedes. When Aeneas's mother, Aphrodite, comes to his aid, Diomedes wounds her too, cutting her wrist and sending her back to Mount Olympus. Aphrodite's mother, Dione, heals her, and Zeus warns Aphrodite not to try her hand at warfare again. When Apollo goes to tend to Aeneas in Aphrodite's stead, Diomedes attacks him as well. This act of aggression breaches Diomedes' agreement with Athena, who had limited him to challenging Aphrodite alone among the gods. Apollo, issuing a stern warning to Diomedes, effortlessly pushes him aside and whisks Aeneas off of the field. Aiming to enflame the passions of Aeneas's comrades, he leaves a replica of Aeneas's body on the ground. He also rouses Ares, god of war, to fight on the Trojan side.

With the help of the gods, the Trojans begin to take the upper hand in battle. Hector and Ares prove too much for the Achaeans; the sight of a hero and god battling side by side frightens even Diomedes. The Trojan Sarpedon kills the Achaean Tlepolemus. Odysseus responds by slaughtering entire lines of Trojans, but Hector cuts down still more Greeks. Finally, Hera and Athena appeal to Zeus, who gives them permission to intervene on the Achaeans' behalf. Hera rallies the rest of the Achaean troops, while Athena encourages Diomedes. She withdraws her earlier injunction not to attack any of the gods except Aphrodite and even jumps in the chariot with him to challenge Ares. The divinely driven chariot charges Ares, and, in the seismic collision that follows, Diomedes wounds

Ares. Ares immediately flies to Mount Olympus and complains to Zeus, but Zeus counters that Ares deserved his injury. Athena and Hera also depart the scene of the battle.

SUMMARY: BOOK 6

With the gods absent, the Achaean forces again overwhelm the Trojans, who draw back toward the city. Menelaus considers accepting a ransom in return for the life of Adrestus, a Trojan he has subdued, but Agamemnon persuades him to kill the man outright. Nestor senses the Trojans weakening and urges the Achaeans not to bother stripping their fallen enemies of their weapons but to focus instead on killing as many as possible while they still have the upper hand. The Trojans anticipate downfall, and the soothsayer Helenus urges Hector to return to Troy to ask his mother, Queen Hecuba, along with her noblewomen, to pray for mercy at the temple of Athena. Hector follows Helenus's advice and gives his mother and the other women their instructions. He then visits his brother Paris, who has withdrawn from battle, claiming he is too grief-stricken to participate. Hector and Helen heap scorn on him for not fighting, and at last he arms himself and returns to battle. Hector also prepares to return but first visits his wife, Andromache, whom he finds nursing their son Astyanax by the walls of the city. As she cradles the child, she anxiously watches the struggle in the plain below. Andromache begs Hector not to go back, but he insists that he cannot escape his fate, whatever it may be. He kisses Astyanax, who, although initially frightened by the crest on Hector's helmet, greets his father happily. Hector then departs. Andromache, convinced that he will soon die, begins to mourn his death. Hector meets Paris on his way out of the city, and the brothers prepare to rejoin the battle.

ANALYSIS: BOOKS 5–6

The battle narratives in Books 5 and 6 (and the very end of Book 4) constitute the epic's first descriptions of warfare, and, within the war as a whole, the first battles in which the sulking Achilles has not fought. Diomedes attempts to make up for the great warrior's absence; the soothsayer Helenus declares, in reference to Diomedes, that "[h]e is the strongest Argive now" (6.115). The Achaeans still feel the consequences of their mightiest soldier's prideful refusal to fight, however, and remain on the defensive for much of Book 5. Even with divine help, Diomedes cannot quite provide the force that

Achilles did. As Hera rightly observes, "As long as brilliant Achilles stalked the front / no Trojan would ever venture beyond the Dardan [Trojan] Gates" (5.907–908). As potent as the rage that Achilles feels toward Agamemnon is his ability to intimidate the Trojans.

Homer communicates the scope and intensity of the battle with long descriptive passages of mass slaughter, yet he intersperses these descriptions with intimate characterization, thereby personalizing the violence. Homer often fleshes out the characters being killed by telling stories about their backgrounds or upbringings. He uses this technique, for instance, when, after Aeneas fells Orsilochus and Crethon midway through Book 5, he recounts the story of how these twins joined up with the Achaean ranks. Furthermore, Homer often alternates between depictions of Trojan and Achaean deaths, sometimes rendering the victor of the first exchange the victim of the next. In this way, he injects a sense of rhythm into what would otherwise be a numbing litany of mass destruction.

The battle narratives also give Homer the chance to comment on the similarities and differences between the mortals and the gods. For while the mortals engage in their armed warfare, the gods engage in their own squabbles. Invariably, the latter conflicts appear less serious, more frivolous, and almost petty. Although the disagreements between the gods sometimes result in further violence among the mortals, as when Athena persuades Pandarus to defy the cease-fire, in Book 4, the gods' loyalties and motivations ultimately emerge as less profound than those of the humans. The gods base their support for one side or the other not on principle but on which heroes they happen to favor. They scheme or make pacts to help one another but often fail to honor these pacts. Ares, for example, though having vowed to support the Achaeans, fights alongside the Trojans throughout Books 5 and 6. Furthermore, when the tide of war doesn't flow in the direction that the gods desire, they whine to Zeus. In contrast with the glorious tragedy of the human conflict, the conflict between the gods has the feel of a dysfunctional family feud.

Perhaps Homer means to comment on the importance of living nobly and bravely: with such fickle gods controlling human fate, one cannot predict how or when death will come; one can only work to make life meaningful in its own right. Hector explains this notion to his wife, Andromache, in their famous encounter, illustrating his perception of what the central issue of the battle is—kleos, or "glory." He knows that his fate is inescapable, but, like all Homeric heroes, he feels compelled to live his life in search of this individual glory.

This encounter also serves to humanize the great warrior Hector: the audience can relate to him as he races, fearing defeat, to his wife and breaks into a grin at the sight of his beloved infant son. Homer achieves such great pathos not only with the words of Hector and Andromache but also with setting and effective detailing. By placing their meeting above the Scaean Gates—the grand entrance to the city, where many confrontations have already occurred—Homer elevates Hector and Andromache's love to the level of the rage that pervades the epic. Homer's use of detail proves similarly crucial to the scene's poignancy. As Andromache nurses baby Astyanax, the audience is reminded of the way in which war separates families and deprives the innocent. When Hector hastily removes his crested helmet upon seeing how it frightens Astyanax, we realize that this great warrior, who has just affirmed his glorious aspirations and his iron will to fight, also possesses a tender side. The scene at once relieves the tension heightened by the descriptions of battle and emphasizes these battles' tragic gravity.

BOOKS 7–8

SUMMARY: BOOK 7

With the return of Hector and Paris the battle escalates, but Apollo and Athena soon decide to end the battle for the day. They plan a duel to stop the present bout of fighting: Hector approaches the Achaean line and offers himself to anyone who will fight him. Only Menelaus has the courage to step forward, but Agamemnon talks him out of it, knowing full well that Menelaus is no match for Hector. Nestor, too old to fight Hector himself, passionately exhorts his comrades to respond to the challenge. Nine Achaeans finally step forward. A lottery is held, and Great Ajax wins.

Hector and Ajax begin their duel by tossing spears, but neither proves successful. They then use their lances, and Ajax draws Hector's blood. The two are about to clash with swords when heralds, spurred by Zeus, call off the fight on account of nightfall. The two heroes exchange gifts and end their duel with a pact of friendship.

That night, Nestor gives a speech urging the Achaeans to ask for a day to bury their dead. He also advises them to build fortifications around their camp. Meanwhile, in the Trojan camp, King Priam makes a similar proposal regarding the Trojan dead. In addition, his son Antenor asks Paris to give up Helen and thereby end the war.

Paris refuses but offers to return all of the loot that he took with her from Sparta. But when the Trojans present this offer to the Achaeans the next day, the Achaeans sense the Trojans' desperation and reject the compromise. Both sides agree, however, to observe a day of respite to bury their respective dead. Zeus and Poseidon watch the Achaeans as they build their fortifications, planning to tear them down as soon as the men leave.

Summary: Book 8

After prohibiting the other gods from interfering in the course of the war, Zeus travels to Mount Ida, overlooking the Trojan plain. There he weighs the fates of Troy and Achaea in his scale, and the Achaean side sinks down. With a shower of lightning upon the Achaean army, Zeus turns the tide of battle in the Trojans' favor, and the Greeks retreat in terror. Riding the Trojans' surge in power, Hector seeks out Nestor, who stands stranded in the middle of the battlefield. Diomedes scoops Nestor into his chariot just in time, and Hector pursues the two of them, intent on driving them all the way to the Greek fortifications, where he plans to set fire to their ships. Hera, seeing the Achaean army collapsing, inspires Agamemnon to rouse his troops. He stirs up their pride, begs them to have heart, and prays for relief from Zeus, who finally sends a sign—an eagle carrying a fawn in its talons. The divine symbol inspires the Achaeans to fight back.

As the Achaeans struggle to regain their power, the archer Teucer fells many Trojans. But Hector finally wounds him, reversing the tide of battle yet again. Hector drives the Greeks behind their fortifications, all the way to their ships. Athena and Hera, unable to bear any further suffering on the part of their favored Greeks, prepare to enter the fray, but Zeus sends the goddess Iris to warn them of the consequences of interfering. Knowing that they cannot compete with Zeus, Athena and Hera relent and return to Mount Olympus. When Zeus returns, he tells them that the next morning will provide their last chance to save the Achaeans. He notes that only Achilles can prevent the Greeks' destruction.

That night, the Trojans, confident in their dominance, camp outside their city's walls, and Hector orders his men to light hundreds of campfires so that the Greeks cannot escape unobserved. Nightfall has saved the Greeks for now, but Hector plans to finish them off the next day.

ANALYSIS

The Achaeans' success so far despite Achilles' absence, along with Paris's cowardice and Hector's hopeless despair in Book 6, have seemed to spell doom for the Trojans. Yet, by the end of Book 8, we recall the Achaeans' bravado with great irony. Hector has nearly seized their ambitious fortifications, and the Trojans appear more determined than ever. The mutual exasperation with the war that motivates the cease-fire of Books 3 and 4 has now disappeared. No longer wanting to end the war, the Trojans desire to win it; that they camp right beside the Achaeans demonstrates their hunger for battle. The severity of the Achaeans' impending loss becomes all too clear in Hector's determination to burn their ships. In a sense, the ships symbolize the future of all Achaea, for although some Achaeans stayed behind in Greece, very few of the land's fathers and sons remain at home. Moreover, the men who have come to Troy constitute the "best of the Achaeans," as the poem continually calls them. Should the Trojans burn their ships, the strongest, noblest men and rulers of the Achaean race would either die in flames or remain stranded on foreign shores.

The catastrophic reversal of the Achaeans' fortune not only adds drama and suspense to the poem but also marks a development in the gods' feuding and aids the progression of the overall plot. Although the gods have involved themselves extensively in the war already, Zeus's entrance into the conflict brings great changes. Whereas he earlier frowns upon the infighting of the other gods but remains aloof himself, he now forbids his fellow Olympians from interfering and plunges headlong into the struggle. The decline of the Achaeans marks not only a change in the gods' behavior but also a more important change in the poem's human dynamics: the Achaeans' eventual collapse motivates their appeal to Achilles in Book 9, which serves to bring the epic's crucial figure to the center of the action. Zeus's statement to Hera that only Achilles can save the Achaeans foreshadows the text's impending focus on the prideful hero. Until now, the reader has witnessed the consequences of Achilles' rage; Book 8 sets the scene for an explosion of his rage onto the battlefield.

Books 7 and 8 give the reader a glimpse of some of the tenets of Greek ritual and belief, which, since Greek culture dominated the ancient Mediterranean world, the Trojan warriors uphold as well. The encounter between Hector and Ajax in Book 7, which ends with them exchanging arms and thereby sealing an unsettled conflict with a pact of friendship, demonstrates the value placed on respect and individual dignity. We see that Greek culture places great significance on both enmity and friendship—on both the taking of lives and the giving of gifts—and that each has its proper place. The characters and the text itself seem to see the proper balancing of these opposites as a manifestation of an individual's worthiness.

Another aspect of the ancient Greek value system emerges in the agreement both sides make to pause their fighting to bury their respective dead. To the Greeks, piety demanded giving the dead, especially those who had died so gloriously, a proper burial, though proper burial could mean a number of things: here the mourners burn the corpses on a pyre; elsewhere they actually bury them. According to ancient Greek belief, only souls whose bodies had been properly disposed of could enter the underworld. To leave a soul unburied, or, worse, to leave it as carrion for wild animals, indicated not only disrespect for the dead individual but, perhaps even worse, disregard for established religious traditions.

BOOKS 9–10

SUMMARY: BOOK 9

> *If I hold out here and I lay siege to Troy,*
> *my journey home is gone, but my glory never dies.*
> (See QUOTATIONS, p. 65)

With the Trojans poised to drive the Achaeans back to their ships, the Achaean troops sit brokenhearted in their camp. Standing before them, Agamemnon weeps and declares the war a failure. He proposes returning to Greece in disgrace. Diomedes rises and insists that he will stay and fight even if everyone else leaves. He buoys the soldiers by reminding them that Troy is fated to fall. Nestor urges perseverance as well, and suggests reconciliation with Achilles. Seeing the wisdom of this idea, Agamemnon decides to offer Achilles a great stockpile of gifts on the condition that he return to the Achaean lines. The king selects some of the Achaeans' best men, including Odysseus, Great Ajax, and Phoenix, to communicate the proposal to Achilles.

The embassy finds Achilles playing the lyre in his tent with his dear friend Patroclus. Odysseus presents Agamemnon's offer, but Achilles rejects it directly. He announces that he intends to return to his homeland of Phthia, where he can live a long, prosaic life instead of the short, glorious one that he is fated to live if he stays. Achilles offers to take Phoenix, who helped rear him in Phthia, with him, but Phoenix launches into his own lengthy, emotional plea for Achilles to stay. He uses the ancient story of Meleager, another warrior who, in an episode of rage, refused to fight, to illustrate the importance of responding to the pleas of helpless friends. But Achilles stands firm, still feeling the sting of Agamemnon's insult. The embassy returns unsuccessful, and the army again sinks into despair.

SUMMARY: BOOK 10

The Greek commanders sleep well that night, with the exception of Agamemnon and Menelaus. Eventually, they rise and wake the others. They convene on open ground, on the Trojan side of their fortifications, to plan their next move. Nestor suggests sending a spy to infiltrate the Trojan ranks, and Diomedes quickly volunteers for the role. He asks for support, and Odysseus steps forward. The two men arm themselves and set off for the Trojan camp. A heron sent by Athena calls out on their right-hand side, and they pray to Athena for protection.

Meanwhile, the Trojans devise their own acts of reconnaissance. Hector wants to know if the Achaeans plan an escape. He selects Dolon, an unattractive but lightning-quick man, to serve as his scout, and promises to reward him with Achilles' chariot and horses once the Achaeans fall. Dolon sets out and soon encounters Diomedes and Odysseus. The two men interrogate Dolon, and he, hoping to save his life, tells them the positions of the Trojans and all of their allies. He reveals to them that the Thracians, newly arrived, are especially vulnerable to attack. Diomedes then kills Dolon and strips him of his armor.

The two Achaean spies proceed to the Thracian camp, where they kill twelve soldiers and their king, Rhesus. They also steal Rhesus's chariot and horses. Athena warns them that some angry god may wake the other soldiers; Diomedes and Odysseus thus ride Rhesus's chariot back to the Achaean camp. Nestor and the other Greeks, worried that their comrades had been killed, greet them warmly.

ANALYSIS: BOOKS 9–10

Although the episodes in Books 9 and 10 take place during the same night, providing a break from the fighting, little continuity exists between them. The mission to Achilles' tent occurs early in the evening, while the mission across the Trojan line occurs quite late—during the third watch, according to Odysseus, or around 3 a.m. The only seeming connection between the two books is the Greeks' desperateness, accentuated by Achilles' obstinacy, which troubles the commanders' sleep and makes them so ready to meet. Despite this lack of continuity, some symmetry nevertheless exists between the two halves of the night. In each case, a meeting of the Achaean command yields a proposal by Nestor to send an expeditionary force to provide the Achaeans with fresh information. Odysseus goes on both expeditions. The mission to Achilles' tent ends in failure, while the mission toward Troy brings success.

Whereas Achilles stews with rage, unwilling to consider the possibility that he might be overreacting to Agamemnon's insulting actions, Agamemnon displays a levelheaded approach to the Achaean dilemma in heeding Nestor's recommendation to reconcile himself with Achilles. "Mad, blind I was! / Not even I deny it," he exclaims, acknowledging his fault in the rift (9.138–139). Yet, despite his seeming eagerness to repair his friendship with Achilles, Agamemnon never issues anything resembling an apology. Though he admits to having been "lost in my own inhuman rage," he seeks to buy back Achilles' loyalty rather than work with him to achieve some mutual understanding of their relationship (9.143). Achilles isn't really seeking an apology, nor does he want simple recompense in the form of wondrous gifts. He wants restitution for the outrage that he has suffered: restoration of the honor and glory for which he has worked so hard and given so much.

While Agamemnon's bountiful offer of sumptuous gifts to Achilles may seem a superficial gesture, it is important to remember that the ancients conceived of material possessions, whether won in battle or awarded by kings, as indicators of personal honor. Nevertheless, though Agamemnon is generous in his offerings, which he believes will "honor [Achilles] like a god," he still essentially calls for Achilles to accept that his status is lower than Agamemnon's (9.185). "Let him bow down to me! I am the greater king," he cries out, illustrating that Agamemnon, though perhaps more pragmatic, is just as self-centered as Achilles (9.192).

The embassy to Achilles constitutes one of the most touching scenes in the *Iliad*. Homer achieves his effect largely through an exchange of narratives, which illuminate Achilles' upbringing and hint at his ultimate fate beyond the scope of the epic. Ostensibly, each side presents these stories to persuade the other side, but Homer uses them to humanize Achilles, to give us a glimpse of his past and future. Although Achilles' pride and rage define the thematic concerns of the epic, they also result in Achilles' absence from most of the action of the poem. Accordingly, Homer has little opportunity to delineate the hero's character. The embassy scene reveals the pressures that Achilles faced in Phthia and highlights the dilemma that he faces now, thus illuminating his inner struggles and thereby making him a richer character.

BOOKS 11–12

SUMMARY: BOOK 11

The next morning, Zeus rains blood upon the Achaean lines, filling them with panic; they suffer a massacre during the first part of the day. But, by afternoon, they have begun to make progress. Agamemnon, splendidly armed, cuts down man after man and beats the Trojans back to the city's gates. Zeus sends Iris to tell Hector that he must wait until Agamemnon is wounded and then begin his attack. Agamemnon soon receives his wound at the hands of Coon, Antenor's son, just after killing Coon's brother. The injured Agamemnon continues fighting and kills Coon, but his pain eventually forces him from the field.

Hector recognizes his cue and charges the Achaean line, driving it back. The Achaeans panic and stand poised to retreat, but the words of Odysseus and Diomedes imbue them with fresh courage. Diomedes then hurls a spear that hits Hector's helmet. This brush with death stuns Hector and forces him to retreat. Paris answers the Achaeans' act by wounding Diomedes with an arrow, thus sidelining the great warrior for the rest of the epic. Trojans now encircle Odysseus, left to fight alone. He beats them all off, but not before a man named Socus gives him a wound through the ribs. Great Ajax carries Odysseus back to camp before the Trojans can harm him further.

Hector resumes his assault on another part of the Achaean line. The Greeks initially hold him off, but they panic when the healer Machaon receives wounds at Paris's hands. Hector and his men force Ajax to retreat as Nestor conveys Machaon back to his tent. Meanwhile, behind the lines, Achilles sees the injured Machaon fly by in a chariot and sends his companion Patroclus to inquire into Machaon's status. Nestor tells Patroclus about all of the wounds that the Trojans have inflicted upon the Achaean commanders. He begs Patroclus to persuade Achilles to rejoin the battle—or at least enter the battle himself disguised in Achilles' armor. This ruse would at least give the Achaeans the benefit of Achilles' terrifying aura. Patroclus agrees to appeal to Achilles and dresses the wound of a man named Eurypylus, who has been injured fighting alongside Ajax.

SUMMARY: BOOK 12

We learn that the Achaean fortifications are doomed to be destroyed by the gods when Troy falls. They continue to hold for now, however, and the trench dug in front of them blocks the Trojan chariots. Undaunted, Hector, acting on the advice of the young commander Polydamas, orders his men to disembark from their chariots and storm the ramparts. Just as the Trojans prepare to cross the trenches, an eagle flies to the left-hand side of the Trojan line and drops a serpent in the soldiers' midst. Polydamas interprets this event as a sign that their charge will fail, but Hector refuses to retreat.

The Trojans Glaucus and Sarpedon now charge the ramparts, and Menestheus, aided by Great Ajax and Teucer, struggles to hold them back. Sarpedon makes the first breach, and Hector follows by shattering one of the gates with a boulder. The Trojans pour through the fortifications as the Achaeans, terrified, shrink back against the ships.

ANALYSIS: BOOKS 11–12

Two instances of divine intervention contribute to an extreme sense of suspense in these scenes. First, Zeus firmly manipulates the battle, from showering the Achaeans with blood to enabling Hector to become the first Trojan to cross the Achaean fortifications. The Achaeans recognize his presence and realize that in fighting the Trojans they pit themselves against the king of the gods. Diomedes even interprets Zeus's acts of favoritism to mean that Zeus has singled out the Trojans for ultimate victory. At the same time, however, the epic frequently reminds us of a second case of divine plotting: according to soothsayers, Troy is fated to fall. Homer builds dramatic tension by juxtaposing this prophecy with vivid descriptions of the Achaeans' sufferings and setbacks. He constantly tempts us with the expectation of Trojan defeat while dashing this prospect with endless examples of the Trojans' success under Zeus's partiality. Ultimately, we feel unable to trust either set of signs.

The frequent reappearance of Zeus also reminds the reader indirectly of Achilles, thus keeping our focus on the *Iliad*'s central conflict. Zeus first enters the war in response to Thetis's prayers and now inflicts the same sort of damage upon the Achaeans that we are led to believe Achilles might easily inflict upon the Trojans if his rage were to abate. Zeus's overpowering of the Achaeans makes Achilles' absence all the more noticeable. Perhaps Homer worries that his audience, like the Achaeans, will miss Achilles—he seems to use the wounding of Machaon, whom Nestor whisks past Achilles' tent toward medical aid, as an opportunity to make Achilles and, perhaps more important, Patroclus appear. The encounter between Nestor and Patroclus does more than present another glimpse of life behind the lines with Achilles and Patroclus; it also sheds some light on the difference in these two men's attitudes. As the text gives information on the background of Patroclus, we begin to wonder whether Patroclus shares Achilles' rage and whether he may wish to rejoin the fight despite his loyalty to his friend.

The scene between Patroclus and Nestor also contains an instance of foreshadowing, hinting at what happens when Patroclus does finally rejoin the battle. Homer writes that Patroclus's "doom [is] sealed" as soon as Achilles calls for him to instruct him to speak with Nestor (11.714). It is Nestor who gives Patroclus the idea of returning to battle dressed in Achilles' armor, by means of which tactic Patroclus meets his death. The reference to Patroclus's doom not only foreshadows Patroclus's end but also points toward the event that finally motivates Achilles himself to return to battle.

BOOKS 13–14

SUMMARY: BOOK 13

Zeus, happy with the war's progress, takes his leave of the battlefield. Poseidon, eager to help the Achaeans and realizing that Zeus has gone, visits Little Ajax and Great Ajax in the form of Calchas and gives them confidence to resist the Trojan assault. He also rouses the rest of the Achaeans, who have withdrawn in tears to the sides of the ships. Their spirits restored, the Achaeans again stand up to the Trojans, and the two Aeantes (the plural of Ajax) prove successful in driving Hector back. When Hector throws his lance at Teucer, Teucer dodges out of the way, and the weapon pierces and kills Poseidon's grandson Amphimachus. As an act of vengeance,

Poseidon imbues Idomeneus with a raging power. Idomeneus then joins Meriones in leading a charge against the Trojans at the Achaeans' left wing. Idomeneus cuts down a number of Trojan soldiers but hopes most of all to kill the warrior Deiphobus. Finding him on the battlefield, he taunts the Trojan, who summons Aeneas and other comrades to his assistance. In the long skirmish that ensues, Deiphobus is wounded, and Menelaus cuts down several Trojans.

Meanwhile, on the right, Hector continues his assault, but the Trojans who accompany him, having been mercilessly battered by the two Aeantes, have lost their vigor. Some have returned to the Trojan side of the fortifications, while those who remain fight from scattered positions. Polydamas persuades Hector to regroup his forces. Hector fetches Paris and tries to gather his comrades from the left end of the line—only to find them all wounded or dead. Great Ajax insults Hector, and an eagle appears on Ajax's right, a favorable omen for the Achaeans.

SUMMARY: BOOK 14

Nestor leaves the wounded Machaon in his tent and goes to meet the other wounded Achaean commanders out by the ships. The men scan the battlefield and realize the terrible extent of their losses. Agamemnon proposes giving up and setting sail for home. Odysseus wheels on him and declares this notion cowardly and disgraceful. Diomedes urges them all to the line to rally their troops. As they set out, Poseidon encourages Agamemnon and gives added strength to the Achaean army.

Hera spots Zeus on Mount Ida, overlooking Troy, and devises a plan to distract him so that she may help the Achaeans behind his back. She visits Aphrodite and tricks her into giving her an enchanted breastband into which the powers of Love and Longing are woven, forceful enough to make the sanest man go mad. She then visits the embodiment of Sleep, and by promising him one of her daughters in marriage, persuades him to lull Zeus to sleep. Sleep follows her to the peak of Mount Ida; disguised as a bird, he hides in a tree. Zeus sees Hera, and the enchanted band seizes him with passion. He makes love to Hera and, as planned, soon falls asleep. Hera then calls to Poseidon, telling him that he now has free reign to steer the Achaeans to victory. Poseidon regroups them, and they charge the Trojans. In the ensuing scuffle, Great Ajax knocks Hector to the ground with a boulder, and the Trojans must carry the hero back to Troy. With Hector gone, the Achaeans soon trounce their enemies, and Trojans die in great numbers as the army flees back to the city.

ANALYSIS: BOOKS 13–14

The scene between Hera and Zeus in Book 14 does little to advance the plot of the poem, as Zeus has already departed the scene of battle and ceased to support the Trojans. However, the scene does provide some comic relief. Once again, it is striking how issues of life and death in the mortal world are so often determined by petty feuds in the godly realms. Here, the decisive turn in the battle results from Zeus's libido and Aphrodite's gullibility, as well as Hera's indignant mischievousness. Time after time, these divinities prove that they are far from always rational and levelheaded, that they are constrained by many of the same emotions and needs as humans. Interestingly, Homer never passes judgment on or questions the gods' temperaments. Instead, he accepts their sensitivities as fundamental to their existence.

Although the Greeks now rise again to power, the troops rally under a temporarily reduced set of leaders. With the exception of the two Aeantes and Menelaus, few of the most familiar Achaean warriors fight in Books 13 and 14. Agamemnon, Odysseus, and Diomedes have all been injured, and Nestor now tends to the wounded healer Machaon; Menelaus appears once, but only briefly. This new focus on Greece's second string affects the narrative in a number of interesting ways. First, it spotlights the Trojan commanders; Hector, Paris, and Aeneas all play significant roles in these two books. Hector's leadership abilities, for instance, come to the foreground as he must decide, with help from Polydamas, first how to divide his army along the Achaean line and second whether to retreat and regroup his forces. Similarly, by keeping less senior commanders in the thick of the fight on the Achaean side, Homer is able to focus on the leadership and tactical skills of the main Achaean characters.

This focus corresponds to the more general attention paid in Books 13 and 14 to the tactical rather than physical aspects of war. The fighting described in these books entails less chaos and more controlled movement between groups of men. Polydamas and Hector discuss which part of the line needs reinforcement, and Poseidon urges the Achaeans to redistribute their arms more efficiently between stronger and weaker soldiers. Even Hera's collaboration with Poseidon and her deception of Zeus and Aphrodite contrast with the brute force that Zeus uses to put the Trojans ahead in Books 8 through 12.

BOOKS 15–16

SUMMARY: BOOK 15

Zeus wakes and sees the havoc that Hera and Poseidon have wreaked while he dozed in his enchanted sleep. Hera tries to blame Poseidon, but Zeus comforts her by making clear that he has no personal interest in a Trojan victory over the Achaeans. He tells her that he will again come to their aid, but that Troy is still fated to fall and that Hector will die after he kills Patroclus. He then asks Hera to summon Iris and Apollo. Iris goes to order Poseidon to leave the battlefield, which Poseidon reluctantly agrees to do, while Apollo seeks out Hector and fills him and his comrades with fresh strength. Hector leads a charge against the Achaeans, and while their leaders initially hold their ground, they retreat in terror when Apollo himself enters the battle. Apollo covers over the trench in front of the Greek fortifications, allowing the Trojans to beat down the ramparts once again.

The armies fight all the way to the ships and very nearly into the Greek camp. At the base of the ships, furious hand-to-hand fighting breaks out. Great Ajax and Hector again tangle. The archer Teucer fells several Trojans, but Zeus snaps his bowstring when he takes aim at Hector. Ajax encourages his troops from the decks of the ships, but Hector rallies the Trojans, and inch by inch the Trojans advance until Hector is close enough to touch a ship.

SUMMARY: BOOK 16

Meanwhile, Patroclus goes to Achilles' tent and begs to be allowed to wear Achilles' armor if Achilles still refuses to rejoin the battle himself. Achilles declines to fight but agrees to the exchange of armor, with the understanding that Patroclus will fight only long enough to save the ships. As Patroclus arms himself, the first ship goes up in flames. Achilles sends his Myrmidon soldiers, who have not been fighting during their commander's absence, out to accompany Patroclus. He then prays to Zeus that Patroclus may return with both himself and the ships unharmed. The poet reveals, however, that Zeus will grant only one of these prayers.

With the appearance of Patroclus in Achilles' armor the battle quickly turns, and the Trojans retreat from the Achaean ships. At first, the line holds together, but when Hector retreats, the rest of the Trojans become trapped in the trenches. Patroclus now slaughters every Trojan he encounters. Zeus considers saving his son

Sarpedon, but Hera persuades him that the other gods would either look down upon him for it or try to save their own mortal offspring in turn. Zeus resigns himself to Sarpedon's mortality. Patroclus soon spears Sarpedon, and both sides fight over his armor. Hector returns briefly to the front in an attempt to retrieve the armor.

Zeus decides to kill Patroclus for slaying Sarpedon, but first he lets him rout the Trojans. Zeus then imbues Hector with a temporary cowardice, and Hector leads the retreat. Patroclus, disobeying Achilles, pursues the Trojans all the way to the gates of Troy. Homer explains that the city might have fallen at this moment had Apollo not intervened and driven Patroclus back from the gates. Apollo persuades Hector to charge Patroclus, but Patroclus kills Cebriones, the driver of Hector's chariot. Trojans and Achaeans fight for Cebriones' armor. Amid the chaos, Apollo sneaks up behind Patroclus and wounds him, and Hector easily finishes him off. Hector taunts the fallen man, but with his dying words Patroclus foretells Hector's own death.

ANALYSIS: BOOKS 15–16

Book 15 marks the beginning of the end for Hector and the Trojans, who have reached the height of their power and now face a downhill slope. From this vantage point, the end is in sight, and, correspondingly, Zeus now outlines the rest of the *Iliad* and beyond, predicting even the eventual fall of Troy, which occurs after the end of the poem. Zeus's speech makes it clear to the reader that a predestined conclusion awaits the Achaeans and Trojans; he is thus able to summarize the story even before the events occur.

This sense of predestination points to an important difference between ancient and modern fiction. Much of modern fiction creates a sense of dramatic tension by keeping the reader wondering how a story will end. Often a story's ending depends upon the individual characters and the choices that they make according to their respective personalities. In contrast, ancient narratives often base themselves on mythological tradition, and ancient audiences would have listened to a given story already aware of its outcome. Tension in this scenario arises not from the question of how a character's mind-set will affect the story's events but rather from the question of how the story's events will affect a character's mindset. For example, the poem creates a sense of drama and poignancy in its portrayal of Hector, who continues to fight valiantly for Troy even though he knows in his heart—as he tells Andromache in Book 6—that he is doomed to die and Troy doomed to fall. Similarly, Achilles eventually rejoins the battle despite his knowledge that the glory of fighting will cost him his life. The drama comes not from waiting to see how the story ends but from waiting to see how the characters respond to an end already foreseen.

Some of the details of the *Iliad*'s plot do depend on individual characters' choices, however. Achilles faces the dilemma of whether to enter the battle and save his comrades or stew in his angry self-pity and let them suffer. These inner struggles of an individual character create not only a sense of drama but often a sense of irony as well. In Book 1, Achilles asks Zeus, via Thetis, to punish the Achaeans for Agamemnon's insolence in demanding the maiden Briseis. Now, as Zeus continues to oblige, helping the Trojans, Achilles loses his beloved comrade Patroclus. In another twist of irony, the death of Patroclus later motivates Achilles to rejoin the Achaean army and lead it against Troy, the very cause that he had forsworn before the beginning of the *Iliad*.

Some commentators detect a change in the characterization of Hector in this part of the epic. Earlier the undisputed champion of the Trojan army who criticizes Paris for retreating, Hector is twice shown fleeing battle after Patroclus's entrance. The Trojan Glaucus shames him into returning the first time, and Hector's uncle shames him into returning the second time (though Homer does point out that Zeus has made Hector cowardly). Additionally, Hector's prediction that he will kill Achilles is empty boasting. Indeed, he can hardly even lay claim to having killed Patroclus, as both Apollo and another Trojan wound Patroclus before Hector can lay a hand on him.

BOOKS 17–18

Summary: Book 17

> *There is nothing alive more agonized than man*
> *of all that breathe and crawl across the earth.*
> (See QUOTATIONS, p. 66)

A fight breaks out over Patroclus's body. Euphorbus, the Trojan who first speared him, tries to strip him of Achilles' armor but is killed by Menelaus. Hector, spurred on by Apollo, sees Euphorbus's fall and comes to help. Menelaus enlists the help of Great Ajax, who forces Hector to back down and prevents the body from being removed or desecrated. He arrives too late to save the armor, however, which Hector dons himself. Glaucus rebukes Hector for leaving Patroclus's body behind and suggests that they might have traded it for Sarpedon's. Hector reenters the fray, promising to give half of the war's spoils to any Trojan who drags Patroclus's corpse away.

Aware of Hector's impending doom and perhaps pitying it, Zeus temporarily gives Hector great power. Ajax and Menelaus summon more Achaeans to help them, and they soon force the Trojans, including mighty Hector, to run for the city's walls. Aeneas, invigorated by Apollo, rallies the fleeing men to return to the fight, but after much effort they remain unable to take the corpse. Achilles' charioteer, Automedon, becomes involved in the fighting as Zeus imbues his team with fresh strength. Hector tries to kill Automedon so that he can steal the chariot, but Automedon dodges Hector's spear and brings a Trojan down in the process. He strips the Trojan of his armor, claiming that in doing so he eases the grief of Patroclus's spirit, though this present victim could hardly compare to the great Patroclus.

Athena, disguised as Phoenix, gives fresh strength to Menelaus, while Apollo, himself disguised as a Trojan, lends encouragement to Hector. Menelaus sends Antilochus for help from Achilles, who still doesn't know of Patroclus's death. Zeus begins moving the battle in the Trojans' favor but relents long enough for Menelaus and Meriones to carry away Patroclus's body.

SUMMARY: BOOK 18

When Antilochus brings word to Achilles of Patroclus's death, Achilles loses control of himself. He weeps and beats the ground with his fists and covers his face with dirt. He utters a "terrible, wrenching cry" so profound that Thetis hears him and comes with her water-nymph sisters from the ocean to learn what troubles her son (18.39). Achilles tells her of the tragedy and insists that he shall avenge himself on Hector, despite his knowledge that, should he choose to live the life of a warrior, he is fated to die young. Thetis responds that since Hector now wears Achilles' armor, she will have the divine metalsmith Hephaestus make him a new set, if Achilles will delay exacting his revenge for one day.

Thetis departs, and Iris, sent by Hera, comes to tell Achilles that he must go outside and make an appearance on the battlefield. This appearance alone will scare the Trojans into abandoning the fight for Patroclus's body. Achilles leaves his tent, accompanied by Athena, and lets loose an enormous cry that does indeed send the Trojans fleeing.

That night, each army holds an assembly to plan its next move. In the Trojan camp, Polydamas urges his comrades to retreat to the city now that Achilles has decided to return to battle. Hector dismisses the idea as cowardly and insists on repeating the previous day's assault. His foolhardy plan wins the support of the Trojans, for Athena has robbed them of their wits. Meanwhile, in the Achaean camp, the men begin their mourning for Patroclus. Achilles has men clean Patroclus's wounds to prepare him for burial, though he vows not to bury him until he has slain Hector. Thetis goes to Hephaestus's mansion and begs him to make Achilles a new set of armor. Hephaestus forges a breastplate, a helmet, and an extraordinary shield embossed with the images of constellations, pastures, dancing children, and cities of men.

ANALYSIS: BOOKS 17–18

In Book 18, night falls for the first time since Book 10; this sunless interlude plays a key role in the pacing, pitch, and drama of the poem, providing a lull in which both the characters and the reader can prepare for the intensity to come. This break from battle also serves to emphasize the significance of Achilles' desire to exact revenge upon Hector; the actions that he soon takes mark his first entry into battle and, simultaneously, the first lessening of his self-pity and pride. By having night fall upon the scene, Homer sets off the imminent episode of Achilles' attempt at revenge from the preceding slaughter. Indeed, Achilles' entry into battle constitutes a metaphoric new dawn for the Achaeans.

The two assemblies held that night contrast sharply with each other, creating a sense of great irony. The Achaeans, still pinned behind their fortifications, mourn a dead comrade and dwell on their woes; yet the next day brings their fatal blow to the Trojan army. Buoyed by the day's success, the Trojans plan a second assault on the Achaean camp, though it is they, not the Achaeans, who will enter into mourning within the next twenty-four hours. The doomed plan's popularity among the Trojans is even more ironic given the availability of Polydamas's wise alternative to retreat into the city. Homer frequently uses the sensible Polydamas as a foil (a character whose emotions or attitudes contrast with and thereby accentuate those of another character) for the headstrong Hector. This technique proves quite effective in this scene. Hector's blindness emerges not only in the formulation of his own foolhardy plan but also in his dismissal of a clearly superior option.

Like the nighttime interlude, the forging of Achilles' new armor helps set a tone of dramatic expectation in the poem. The magnificence of the armor's beauty seems to bespeak its equally magnificent strength. The language describing the shield proves especially compelling and constitutes an example of the literary device *ekphrasis*. *Ekphrasis*, a Greek word literally meaning "description," refers to the description of visual art in poetic terms. This device effectively allows Homer to filter an artistic subject through two layers of imaginative rendering. In the case of Achilles' shield, the use of *ekphrasis* allows Homer to portray poetically not only the images appearing on the metal but also the effect of those images. For example, figures embossed on a shield cannot really move, of course, but Homer portrays them as dancing spiritedly. By doubling up two artistic media—artistic etching and poetry—Homer endows the described images with an enhanced dynamism and aesthetic force. The *ekphrasis* here also serves to create a sense of contrast in the poem. The *Iliad* is a highly compact narrative, compressing the turning points of a ten-year conflict into a few days of battle. Yet the shield passage expands this setting to a timeless universe. At this moment, the poet stands back from the details of physical violence and personal vendettas to contemplate the beauty of the larger cosmos in which they take place.

BOOKS 19–20

SUMMARY: BOOK 19

Thetis presents Achilles with the armor that Hephaestus has forged for him. She promises to look after Patroclus's body and keep it from rotting while Achilles goes to battle. Achilles walks along the shore, calling his men to an assembly. At the meeting, Agamemnon and Achilles reconcile with each other, and Agamemnon gives Achilles the gifts that he promised him should Achilles ever return to battle. He also returns Briseis.

Achilles announces his intention to go to war at once. Odysseus persuades him to let the army eat first, but Achilles himself refuses to eat until he has slain Hector. All through breakfast, he sits mourning his dear friend Patroclus and reminiscing. Even Briseis mourns, for Patroclus had treated her kindly when she was first led away from her homeland. Zeus finds the scene emotionally moving and sends Athena down to fill Achilles' stomach with nectar and ambrosia, keeping his hunger at bay. Achilles then dons his armor and mounts his chariot. As he does so, he chastises his horses, Roan Beauty and Charger, for leaving Patroclus on the battlefield to die. Roan Beauty replies that it was not he but a god who let Patroclus die and that the same is fated for Achilles. But Achilles needs no reminders of his fate; he knows his fate already, and knows that by entering battle for his friend he seals his destiny.

SUMMARY: BOOK 20

While the Achaeans and Trojans prepare for battle, Zeus summons the gods to Mount Olympus. He knows that if Achilles enters the battlefield unchecked, he will decimate the Trojans and maybe even bring the city down before its fated time. Accordingly, he thus removes his previous injunction against divine interference in the battle, and the gods stream down to earth. But the gods soon decide to watch the fighting rather than involve themselves in it, and they take their seats on opposite hills overlooking the battlefield, interested to see how their mortal teams will fare on their own.

Before he resigns himself to a passive role, however, Apollo encourages Aeneas to challenge Achilles. The two heroes meet on the battlefield and exchange insults. Achilles is about to stab Aeneas fatally when Poseidon, in a burst of sympathy for the Trojan—and much to the chagrin of the other, pro-Greek gods—whisks Aeneas away. Hector then approaches, but Apollo persuades him not to strike up a duel in front of the ranks but rather to wait with the other soldiers until Achilles comes to him. Hector initially obeys, but when he sees Achilles so smoothly slaughtering the Trojans, among them one of Hector's brothers, he again challenges Achilles. The fight goes poorly for Hector, and Apollo is forced to save him a second time.

ANALYSIS: BOOKS 19–20

Although Achilles has reconciled with Agamemnon, his other actions in Books 19 and 20 indicate that he has made little progress as a character. He still demonstrates a tendency toward the thoughtless rage that has brought so many Achaeans to their deaths. He remains so intent on vengeance, for example, that he initially intends for the men to go into battle without food, which could prove suicidal in a form of warfare that involves such great expenditures of physical energy. Similarly, on the battlefield Achilles demonstrates an obsessive concern with victory—to the exclusion of all other considerations. He cuts down the Trojan Tros even though Tros supplicates him and begs to be saved; it is apparent that Achilles has done little soul-searching. Although he reconciles himself with the Achaean forces, this gesture doesn't alleviate his rage but rather refocuses it. He now lashes out at the Trojans, expressing his anger through action rather than through pointed refusals to act. Burning with passion, Achilles rejects all appeals to cool-headed reflection; the text compares him to an "inhuman fire" and, when he dons his shining armor, likens him to the sun (20.554). This imagery recalls his portrayal in Book 1 as "blazing Achilles" (1.342).

Indeed, Achilles' internal dilemma as a character remains largely the same as in the beginning of the epic. Achilles has known throughout that his fate is either to live a short, glorious life at Troy or a long, obscure life back in Phthia. Now, as before, he must choose between them. Although he still feels torn between the two options, the shock of Patroclus's death has shifted the balance in favor of remaining at Troy. There is little reason to believe that Achilles would have made up his mind without such a powerful catalyst for his decision.

These books of the poem concern themselves not only with the motivations and consequences of characters' actions but also with the forces at work outside direct human agency. In particular, Agamemnon speaks of the powers of Zeus and Fate, blaming them for his stubbornness in the quarrel with Achilles. He notes that many have held him responsible for the destruction that his insult to Achilles has caused, but he insists that his earlier "savage madness" was driven into his heart by force (19.102). He also cites the force of "Ruin," a translation of the Greek word Ate, which refers to delusion and madness as well as to the disaster that such mental states can bring about (19.106). But Agamemnon and other characters throughout the epic describe Ruin not as a mortal phenomenon but as something external to human psychology; ruin is described as a sentient being in and of itself. In Book 9, for example, Peleus describes Ruin as a woman, "strong and swift," coursing over the earth wreaking havoc (9.614). Here, Agamemnon refers to Ruin as Zeus's daughter, gliding over the earth with delicate feet, entangling men one by one, and even proving capable of entangling Zeus himself.

Another force repeatedly invoked here and throughout the *Iliad* is Fate. Despite the constant references to it, however, we never attain a clear sense of Fate's properties. The first few lines of the poem suggest that the will of Zeus overpowers all, yet at times Zeus himself seems beholden to Fate. In Book 15, for example, he agrees to cease his aid to the Trojans because he knows that Troy is fated to fall. At other times, Zeus and Fate appear to work cooperatively, as in Book 20, when Zeus rallies the gods to stop Achilles from sacking Troy before its fated time. But one wonders to what extent this Fate is really fate at all, if Achilles can so easily preempt it. Other questions arise in Poseidon's discussion of Fate, for he justifies saving Aeneas from Achilles on the grounds that Aeneas is fated to live. This reasoning is paradoxical, for if Aeneas is fated to live, he should not need rescuing.

Ultimately, the *Iliad* doesn't present a clear hierarchy of the cosmic powers; we are left uncertain as to whether the gods control Fate or are forced to follow its dictates. The external forces of Fate, Ruin, and the gods remain as obscure as the inner workings of the human psyche. Thus, while the poet and his characters may attribute certain events to a personified Fate or Fury, such ascriptions do little to explain the events. Indeed, they achieve quite the opposite effect, indicating the mysterious nature of the universe and the human actions within it. To invoke Ruin or the gods is to suggest not only that certain aspects of our world lie beyond human control but also that many phenomena lie beyond human understanding as well.

BOOKS 21–22

SUMMARY & ANALYSIS

SUMMARY: BOOK 21

Achilles routs the Trojans and splits their ranks, pursuing half of them into the river known to the gods as Xanthus and to the mortals as Scamander. On the riverbank, Achilles mercilessly slaughters Lycaon, a son of Priam. The Trojan Asteropaeus, given fresh strength by the god of the river, makes a valiant stand, but Achilles kills him as well. The vengeful Achilles has no intention of sparing any Trojans now that they have killed Patroclus. He throws so many corpses into the river that its channels become clogged. The river god rises up and protests, and Achilles agrees to stop throwing people into the water but not to stop killing them. The river, sympathetic to the Trojans, calls for help from Apollo, but when Achilles hears the river's plea, he attacks the river. The river gets the upper hand and drags Achilles all the way downstream to a floodplain. He very nearly kills Achilles, but the gods intervene. Hephaestus, sent by Hera, sets the plain on fire and boils the river until he relents.

A great commotion now breaks out among the gods as they watch and argue over the human warfare. Athena defeats Ares and Aphrodite. Poseidon challenges Apollo, but Apollo refuses to fight over mere mortals. His sister Artemis taunts him and tries to encourage him to fight, but Hera overhears her and pounces on her.

Meanwhile, Priam sees the human carnage on the battlefield and opens the gates of Troy to his fleeing troops. Achilles pursues them and very nearly takes the city, but the Trojan prince Agenor challenges him to single combat. Achilles' fight with Agenor—and with Apollo disguised as Agenor after Agenor himself has been whisked to safety—allows the Trojans enough time to scurry back to Troy.

SUMMARY: BOOK 22

Hector now stands as the only Trojan left outside Troy. Priam, overlooking the battlefield from the Trojan ramparts, begs him to come inside, but Hector, having given the overconfident order for the Trojans to camp outside their gates the night before, now feels too ashamed to join them in their retreat. When Achilles finally returns from chasing Apollo (disguised as Agenor), Hector confronts him. At first, the mighty Trojan considers trying to negotiate with Achilles, but he soon realizes the hopelessness of his cause and flees. He runs around the city three times, with Achilles at his heels. Zeus considers saving Hector, but Athena persuades him that the mortal's time has come. Zeus places Hector's and Achilles' respective fates on a golden scale, and, indeed, Hector's sinks to the ground.

During Hector's fourth circle around the city walls, Athena appears before him, disguised as his ally Deiphobus, and convinces him that together they can take Achilles. Hector stops running and turns to face his opponent. He and Achilles exchange spear throws, but neither scores a hit. Hector turns to Deiphobus to ask him for a lance; when he finds his friend gone, he realizes that the gods have betrayed him. In a desperate bid for glory, he charges Achilles. However, he still wears Achilles' old armor—stolen from Patroclus's dead body—and Achilles knows the armor's weak points intimately. With a perfectly timed thrust he puts his spear through Hector's throat. Near death, Hector pleads with Achilles to return his body to the Trojans for burial, but Achilles resolves to let the dogs and scavenger birds maul the Trojan hero.

The other Achaeans gather round and exultantly stab Hector's corpse. Achilles ties Hector's body to the back of his chariot and drags it through the dirt. Meanwhile, up above on the city's walls,

King Priam and Queen Hecuba witness the devastation of their son's body and wail with grief. Andromache hears them from her chamber and runs outside. When she sees her husband's corpse being dragged through the dirt, she too collapses and weeps.

ANALYSIS: BOOKS 21–22

In this section of the epic, the feuds of the gods continue to echo the battles of the mortals. As the human battles become ever more grave, however, the divine conflicts in these episodes seem ever more superfluous. In their internal fighting, the gods do not affect or even try to affect the underlying issues of the human conflict. Two of them explicitly swear off fighting over the mortals, though one of these, Hera, ends up doing just that. It seems that the gods are not actually fighting over the mortals but rather expressing the animosities that the mortal conflict has stirred in them. Although the struggle among the gods may remain unexplained within the plot of the epic, it adds variety to the poem's rhythm and pacing, and elevates the conflict onto the epic, cosmos-consuming stage.

But these more lighthearted or colorful episodes soon give way to one of the poem's most deadly serious encounters, the duel between Hector and Achilles. Homer uses several devices, including prophecy and irony, to build a heavy sense of pathos. Priam's speech comparing the glorious death of a hero with the humiliating death of an old man in a fallen city comes across as particularly heartbreaking if we know, as Homer's audience did, that Priam himself will soon meet the very death that he describes, amid the ruins of Troy. When Andromache bewails the miserable life that Astyanax will have to endure without a father, a sharp sense of irony enhances the tragic effect of her words: Astyanax will suffer this fatherless life only briefly, as he dies shortly after the fall of Troy.

This section of the poem reveals a particularly skillful control of plot. Events interweave with one another in elaborate patterns. The weighing of Hector's and Achilles' fates, for example, recalls but inverts the first weighing of fates in Book 8, when the Trojan army's fate rises above that of the Achaeans. Hector must fight to the death in these episodes in order to redeem the honor that he loses earlier; after he recklessly orders his troops to camp outside the city walls, the men have to flee, causing Hector great shame. Furthermore, Hector's earlier moment of glory, when he strips Patroclus of Achilles' armor, speeds the moment of his undoing, for Achilles knows exactly where that armor is vulnerable. Such interconnections between events seem to indicate that the universe has a cyclical or balanced nature: one swing of the pendulum leads to another, and an individual's actions come back to haunt him.

The final duel between Achilles and Hector becomes not only a duel of heroes but also of heroic values. While Achilles proves superior to Hector in terms of strength and endurance, he emerges as inferior in terms of integrity. His mistreatment of Hector's body is a disgrace, compounded by the cruelty in which he allows the rank and file of his army to indulge. As we have seen, Achilles engages in such indignities quite routinely and does so not out of any real principle but out of uncontrollable rage. Hector, on the other hand, entirely redeems whatever flaws he displays in the preceding books. His refusal to return to the safety of Troy's walls after witnessing the deaths brought about by his foolish orders to camp outside the city demonstrates his mature willingness to suffer the consequences of his actions. His rejection of a desperate attempt at negotiation in favor of the honorable course of battle reveals his ingrained sense of personal dignity. His attempt to secure from Achilles a mutual guarantee that the winner treat the loser's corpse with respect highlights his decency. Finally, his last stab at glory by charging Achilles even after he learns that the gods have abandoned him and that his death is imminent makes his heroism and courage obvious. While Hector dies in this scene, the values that he represents—nobility, self-restraint, and respect—arguably survive him. Indeed, Achilles later comes around to an appreciation of these very values after realizing the faults of his earlier brutality and self-centered rage.

BOOKS 23–24

SUMMARY: BOOK 23

At the Achaean camp, Achilles and the Myrmidons continue their mourning for Patroclus. Achilles finally begins to accept food, but he still refuses to wash until he has buried Patroclus. That night, his dead companion appears to him in a dream, begging Achilles to hold his funeral soon so that his soul can enter the land of the dead. The next day, after an elaborate ceremony in which he sacrifices the Achaeans' twelve Trojan captives, Achilles prays for assistance from the winds and lights Patroclus's funeral pyre.

The day after, following the burial of Patroclus's bones, Achilles holds a series of competitions in Patroclus's honor. Marvelous prizes are offered, and both the commanders and the soldiers compete. The events include boxing, wrestling, archery, and a chariot race, which Diomedes wins with some help from Athena. Afterward, Achilles considers stripping the prize from the second-place finisher, Antilochus, to give as consolation to the last-place finisher, whom Athena has robbed of victory so that Diomedes would win. But Antilochus becomes furious at the idea of having his prize taken from him. Menelaus then adds to the argument, declaring that Antilochus committed a foul during the race. After some heated words, the men reconcile with one another.

Summary: Book 24

> *Remember your own father, great godlike Achilles—*
> *as old as I am, past the threshold of deadly old age!*
> (See QUOTATIONS, p. 67)

Achilles continues mourning Patroclus and abusing Hector's body, dragging it around his dead companion's tomb. Apollo, meanwhile, protects Hector's corpse from damage and rot and staves off dogs and scavengers. Finally, on the twelfth day after Hector's death, Apollo persuades Zeus that Achilles must let Hector's body be ransomed. Zeus sends Thetis to bring the news to Achilles, while Iris goes to Priam to instruct him to initiate the ransom. Hecuba fears that Achilles will kill her husband, but Zeus reassures her by sending an eagle as a good omen.

Priam sets out with his driver, Idaeus, and a chariot full of treasure. Zeus sends Hermes, disguised as a benevolent Myrmidon soldier, to guide Priam through the Achaean camp. When the chariot arrives at Achilles' tent, Hermes reveals himself and then leaves Priam alone with Achilles. Priam tearfully supplicates Achilles, begging for Hector's body. He asks Achilles to think of his own father, Peleus, and the love between them. Achilles weeps for his father and for Patroclus. He accepts the ransom and agrees to give the corpse back.

That night, Priam sleeps in Achilles' tent, but Hermes comes to him in the middle of the night and rouses him, warning him that he must not sleep among the enemy. Priam and Idaeus wake, place Hector in their chariot, and slip out of the camp unnoticed. All of the women in Troy, from Andromache to Helen, cry out in grief when they first see Hector's body. For nine days the Trojans prepare Hector's funeral pyre—Achilles has given them a reprieve from battle. The Trojans light Hector's pyre on the tenth day.

ANALYSIS: BOOKS 23–24

The games at Patroclus's funeral serve primarily as a buffer between two climactic events—the death of Hector and his burial. Accordingly, they serve little purpose in the story's plot. Some of the competitions, however, especially the chariot race, provide some drama, but none of the events of Book 24 hinge on their outcome. In a scene that strongly echoes the incident that provokes Achilles' initial rage at Agamemnon, Achilles—ironically—tries to strip the second-place charioteer, Antilochus, of his rightfully won prize. Just as Antilochus finishes second to Diomedes, so does Achilles rank second to Agamemnon; Antilochus, as Achilles does earlier, refuses to suffer the injustice and humiliation of having his achievements go unappreciated. Unlike the conflict between Achilles and Agamemnon, however, this matter is settled peacefully and has no lasting results for any of the characters. Ultimately, the games function for the reader much as they do for the characters—as a diversion from grief.

The *Iliad* ends much as it began: just as Chryses does in Book 1, Priam now crosses enemy lines to supplicate the man who has his child. This time, however, the father's prayers are immediately granted. Priam's invocation of Achilles' own father, Peleus, forges a momentary bond between him and Achilles. Achilles knows that he is fated never to return to Phthia, meaning that one day Peleus will be the bereft father that Achilles has made Priam, mourning a child snatched from his grasp in enemy territory. This realization that his own father is doomed to suffer what Priam is now suffering finally melts Achilles' rage, bringing a sense of closure to the poem.

The bond between Achilles and Priam proves entirely transitory, however. No alliances have shifted; Agamemnon would surely take Priam prisoner if he found him in the Achaean camp. Achilles and Priam remain enemies, as Hermes soon reminds Priam. Achilles' first loyalty is still to Patroclus, as he needs to remind himself after giving up the body of Patroclus's murderer. The fate of Troy is still sealed, a city destined to fall violently at the hands of the Achaeans, as Andromache reminds us when she sees Hector's body being carried into the city. Nonetheless, while Achilles and Priam remain enemies, their animosity has become a nobler, more respectful one.

This change seems to stem from the development of Achilles' character. Having begun the epic as a temperamental, prideful, selfish, and impulsive man, Achilles shows himself in Book 24 to possess a sense of sympathy for others. Throughout the poem, Homer charts Achilles' inability to think beyond himself—his wounded pride makes him stubbornly allow the other Achaeans to suffer defeat, and his rage at Patroclus's death makes him utterly disrespect the noble Hector's corpse. Now, however, Achilles not only respects Priam's plea by returning Hector's body but also allows the Trojan people a reprieve from battle in order to honor and grieve their hero thoroughly and properly.

That Achilles' change of heart occasions the poem's conclusion emphasizes the centrality of Achilles' rage to the poem. Homer chooses to conclude the *Iliad* not with the death of Achilles or the fall of Troy but rather with the withering of Achilles' mighty wrath. The lack of emphasis given to dramatic climax in favor of an exploration of human emotion complements the poem's anticlimactic nature as a whole. Homer's audience would have been very familiar with the plot's outcome, and even a modern audience learns relatively early on how things turn out; because the element of suspense is gone, it makes perfect sense for the poem to wrap itself up when its original conflict—Achilles' rage at Agamemnon—has been suitably resolved.

SUMMARY & ANALYSIS

IMPORTANT QUOTATIONS EXPLAINED

1. Rage—Goddess, sing the rage of Peleus' son Achilles,
    murderous, doomed, that cost the Achaeans countless losses,
    hurling down to the House of Death so many sturdy souls,
    great fighters' souls, but made their bodies carrion,
    feasts for the dogs and birds,
    and the will of Zeus was moving toward its end.
    Begin, Muse, when the two first broke and clashed,
    Agamemnon lord of men and brilliant Achilles.

The first lines of an ancient epic poem typically offer a capsule summary of the subject the poem will treat, and the first lines of the *Iliad* conform to this pattern. Indeed, Homer announces his subject in the very first word of the very first line: "Rage." He then locates the rage within "Peleus' son Achilles," delineates its consequences ("cost the Achaeans countless losses . . ."), links it to higher forces and agendas ("the will of Zeus"), and notes its origin (when "the two first broke and clashed, / Agamemnon . . . and brilliant Achilles"). Interestingly, although these lines purport to focus on a human emotion, they interpret this emotion as unfolding in accordance with the expression of Zeus's will. Similarly, Homer conceives of the entire epic as the medium through which a divine being—a Muse—speaks.

As evident in this passage, the poem emphatically does not undertake to deal with the Trojan War as a whole. The poet does not even mention Troy here, and he specifically asks the Muse to begin the story at the time when Agamemnon and Achilles first "broke and clashed"—nine years into the ten-year conflict. Nor does he mention the fall of Troy or the Greek victory, referring only to a vague "end" toward which Zeus's will moves. This does not mean that the Trojan War does not play an important role in the poem. Homer clearly uses the war not just as a setting but as a wellspring for the value system he celebrates, and a source of telling illustrations for his statements on life, death, and fate. Nonetheless, the poem remains fundamentally focused on the conflict within a single man, and this opening passage conveys this focus to the reader.

2.　　We everlasting gods . . . Ah what chilling blows
　　　we suffer—thanks to our own conflicting wills—
　　　whenever we show these mortal men some kindness.

Ares voices this lament after being wounded by Diomedes in Book 5.
His plaint concisely captures the Homeric relationship between gods
and men and, perhaps, Homer's attitude toward that relationship.
Homeric gods frequently intervene in the mortal world out of some
kind of emotional attachment to the object of that intervention.
Here, Ares describes this emotion as simply a desire to do "kindness," but kindness toward one mortal often translates into unkind-
ness toward another—hence Ares' wound at the hands of Diomedes.

　　Divine intervention in the *Iliad* causes conflicts not only in the
mortal sphere but between the gods as well. Each god favors different men, and when these men are at war, divine wars often rage as
well. Ares thus correctly attributes the gods' "chilling blows" to
their "own conflicting wills."

　　Ares' whining does not make him unique among the gods.
Homer's immortals expect to govern according to their wills, which
are in turn governed by self-interest. Correspondingly, they com-
plain when they do not get their way. Ares' melodramatic and self-
pitying lament, which is greeted with scorn by Zeus a few lines later,
probably implies some criticism of the gods by Homer. Ares'
appearance here as a kind of spoiled child provides just one example
of Homer's portrayal of the gods as temperamental, sulky, vengeful,
and petty—a portrayal that may seek to describe and explain the
inequities and absurdities in life on earth.

3.   Cattle and fat sheep can all be had for the raiding,
tripods all for the trading, and tawny-headed stallions.
But a man's life breath cannot come back again—

. . .

            Mother tells me,
the immortal goddess Thetis with her glistening feet,
that two fates bear me on to the day of death.
If I hold out here and I lay siege to Troy,
my journey home is gone, but my glory never dies.
If I voyage back to the fatherland I love,
my pride, my glory dies. . . .

With these words in Book 9, Achilles rejects the embassy of Achaean commanders come to win him back to the war effort. His response here shows that Agamemnon's effrontery—which he discusses earlier in his speech—does not constitute the sole reason for his refusal to fight. Achilles also fears the consequences in store for him if he remains in Troy. His mother, Thetis, has told him that fate has given him two options—either live a short but glorious life in Troy or return to Phthia and live on in old age but obscurity. As he confronts this choice, the promise of gifts and plunder—cattle, fat sheep, stallions—doesn't interest him at all. Such material gifts can be traded back and forth, or even taken away, as his prize Briseis was. In contrast, the truly precious things in the world are those that cannot be bought, sold, seized, or commodified in any way. These include glory and life itself.

    The choice that Achilles must make in this scene is between glory and life; it is not merely a matter of whether to accept the gifts or to continue protesting Agamemnon's arrogance. At this point in the epic, Achilles has chosen life over glory, and he explains that he plans to return to Phthia. However, the allure of glory later proves irresistible when he finds a compelling occasion for it—avenging the death of his beloved friend Patroclus.

QUOTATIONS

4.   There is nothing alive more agonized than man
      of all that breathe and crawl across the earth.

Zeus speaks these words to the horses of Achilles' chariot, who
weep over the death of Patroclus in Book 17. Grim as they are, the
lines accurately reflect the Homeric view of the human condition.
Throughout the *Iliad,* as well as the *Odyssey,* mortals often figure as
little more than the playthings of the gods. Gods can whisk them
away from danger as easily as they can put them in the thick of it. It
is thus appropriate that the above lines are spoken by a god, and not
by a mortal character or the mortal poet; the gods know the mortals'
agony, as they play the largest role in causing it.

    While gods can presumably manipulate and torment other ani-
mals that "breathe and crawl across the earth," humanity's con-
sciousness of the arbitrariness of their treatment at the hands of the
gods, their awareness of the cruel choreography going on above,
increases their agony above that of all other creatures. For while the
humans remain informed of the gods' interventions, they remain
powerless to contradict them. Moreover, humans must deal with a
similarly fruitless knowledge of their fates. The *Iliad's* two most
important characters, Achilles and Hector, both know that they are
doomed to die early deaths. Hector knows in addition that his city is
doomed to fall, his brothers and family to be extinguished, and his
wife to be reduced to slavery. These men's agony arises from the fact
that they bear the burden of knowledge without being able to use
this knowledge to bring about change.

5.   Remember your own father, great godlike Achilles—
        as old as I am, past the threshold of deadly old age!
        No doubt the countrymen round about him plague him now,
        with no one there to defend him, beat away disaster.
        No one—but at least he hears you're still alive
        and his old heart rejoices, hopes rising, day by day,
        to see his beloved son come sailing home from Troy.

With these words, spoken in the middle of Book 24, Priam implores Achilles to return Hector's corpse for proper burial. He makes himself sympathetic in Achilles' eyes by drawing a parallel between himself and Achilles' father, Peleus. Priam imagines Peleus surrounded by enemies with no one to protect him—a predicament that immediately mirrors his own, as a supplicant standing in the middle of the enemy camp. Moreover, the two fathers' situations resemble each other on a broader scale as well. Hector was the bulwark for Priam's Troy just as Achilles was the bulwark for his father's kingdom back in Phthia, and with the two sons gone, Priam's enemies—the Achaeans—will now close in on him just as those of Peleus will. Priam claims that the parallel fails in only one respect: Peleus can at least hope that his son will come home one day.

    But it is this one alleged hole in Priam's comparison that truly summons Achilles' pity and breaks down his resistance, for, unknown to Priam, Peleus is also destined never to see his son again. Achilles knows, as Priam does not, that he is fated to die at Troy and never return home to Phthia. He realizes that one day Peleus will learn that his son has died at the hands of enemies and that he will never see his body again, just as might happen to Priam if Achilles doesn't return Hector's corpse to him. Priam's comparison turns out to be more true than he knows.

QUOTATIONS

Key Facts

FULL TITLE
The Iliad

AUTHOR
Homer

TYPE OF WORK
Poem

GENRE
Epic

LANGUAGE
Ancient Greek

TIME AND PLACE WRITTEN
Unknown, but probably mainland Greece, around 750 B.C.

DATE OF FIRST PUBLICATION
Unknown

PUBLISHER
Unknown

NARRATOR
The poet, who declares himself to be the medium through which one or many of the Muses speak

POINT OF VIEW
The narrator speaks in the third person. An omniscient narrator (he has access to every character's mind), he frequently gives insight into the thoughts and feelings of even minor characters, gods and mortals alike.

TONE
Awe-inspired, ironic, lamenting, pitying

TENSE
Past

SETTING (TIME)
Bronze Age (around the twelfth or thirteenth century B.C.); the *Iliad* begins nine years after the start of the Trojan War

SETTING (PLACE)
Troy (a city in what is now northwestern Turkey) and its immediate environs

PROTAGONIST
Achilles

MAJOR CONFLICT
Agamemnon's demand for Achilles' war prize, the maiden Briseis, wounds Achilles' pride; Achilles' consequent refusal to fight causes the Achaeans to suffer greatly in their battle against the Trojans.

RISING ACTION
Hector's assault on the Achaean ships; the return of Patroclus to combat; the death of Patroclus

CLIMAX
Achilles' return to combat turns the tide against the Trojans once and for all and ensures the fated fall of Troy to which the poet has alluded throughout the poem.

FALLING ACTION
The retreat of the Trojan army; Achilles' revenge on Hector; the Achaeans' desecration of Hector's corpse

THEMES
The glory of war; military values over family life; the impermanence of human life and its creations

MOTIFS
Armor; burial; fire

SYMBOLS
The Achaean ships; the shield of Achilles

FORESHADOWING
Foreshadowing is prominent in the *Iliad*, as the poet constantly refers to events that have yet to occur and to fated outcomes. Patroclus's return to battle foreshadows Achilles' return to battle, for example, and Hector's taunting of the dead Patroclus foreshadows the desecration of his own corpse by Achilles. Also, Achilles and Hector themselves make references to their own fates—about which they have been informed; technically, only Hector's references foreshadow any event in the poem itself, however, as Achilles dies after the close of the epic.

STUDY QUESTIONS & ESSAY TOPICS

STUDY QUESTIONS

1. *Nestor seems like a minor character in the* Iliad, *but he actually plays a significant role in the development of the epic's plot. What are some of the ways in which the aged king propels the action of the story? What effect does he have on the epic as a whole?*

In his role as storyteller and counselor to the Achaean forces, Nestor often provides motivation for the *Iliad's* plot. He convinces the Achaean army to build fortifications around its ships—fortifications that serve as a locus for much of the future confrontation between the two armies. He proposes the spy mission on which Odysseus and Diomedes kill Dolon and a number of Thracian soldiers. Furthermore, it is Nestor who convinces Agamemnon to send an embassy to Achilles, begging him to return to battle. Although this mission ultimately fails, it provides Homer with the occasion to develop the character of Achilles, giving an important context to his decision to abandon the war effort. Finally, Nestor proposes to have Patroclus fight in Achilles' place wearing his armor. This scheme proves the turning point for the entire epic.

2.   *What is the role of women in the* Iliad? *Does the poem contain any strong female characters, or do the acts and deeds of males dominate the work?*

The *Iliad* certainly contains strong female characters. Athena and Hera rank among the most powerful forces in the book. Even the other male gods cannot stand up to them, and Ares, supposedly the god of war, must cede to Athena's superior might on two occasions. Moreover, Athena and Hera are more than just assertive and forceful. They are cunning, quick-witted, and sharp-tongued. By using her womanly assets and a little trickery, Hera incapacitates even Zeus, the king of gods and men.

In the mortal sphere, however, the *Iliad* has little to offer in the way of strong female figures. Very few women enter the story at all, and the women who do appear usually fall into one of two categories: property, such as Chryseis and Briseis, or interlocutors for male characters, such as Helen and Andromache. Homer uses Helen to reveal the cowardly underside of Paris's character and to spotlight the Achaean commanders when she describes them to Priam on the Trojan ramparts. Andromache helps to make Hector a sympathetic character and provides the stimulus for his speech in Book 6 about the fate of Troy. Thus, the significance of both women lies not in themselves but in the ways they illuminate the men around them. The two may seem to be important characters because of the high status they enjoy relative to other women, but compared to the *Iliad*'s warriors they are little more than props.

3.   *What role does fate play in the emotional and
      psychological effect of the* Iliad? *Why does Homer make
      his characters aware of their impending dooms?*

Homer's original audience would already have been intimately
familiar with the story the *Iliad* tells. Making his characters cogni-
zant of their fates merely puts them on par with the epic's audience.
In deciding to make his characters knowledgeable about their own
futures, he loses the effect of dramatic irony, in which the audience
watches characters stumble toward ends that it alone knows in
advance. But Homer doesn't sacrifice drama; in fact, this technique
renders the characters more compelling. They do not fall to ruin out
of ignorance, but instead become tragic figures who go knowingly
to their doom because they have no real choice. In the case of Hector
and Achilles, their willing submission to a fate they recognize but
cannot evade renders them not only tragic but emphatically heroic.

SUGGESTED ESSAY TOPICS

1. Is there a "heroic code" that guides the decisions of the characters in the *Iliad*? Discuss the values of the Homeric hero, paying particular attention to contrasting characters such as Achilles, Odysseus, Paris, and Hector. Does one character emerge as more heroic than the rest? Does one character emerge as less heroic?

2. Discuss Homer's portrayal of the gods in the *Iliad*. What is their relationship with mortals? With fate? Why might Homer have chosen the gods as a frequent source of comic relief? What larger points does Homer seem to be making by depicting the gods as he does?

3. With particular attention to Priam and Hector, as well as to Achilles and Peleus, discuss how the *Iliad* portrays relationships between fathers and sons. In what way does ancestral loyalty affect the characters' behavior? You may want to consider the encounter between Diomedes and Glaucus as well. How do relationships between fathers and sons differ from those between mothers and sons?

4. Does Achilles ultimately emerge as a sympathetic character? Why or why not? Use examples from the text to explain your answer.

Review & Resources

Quiz

1. Who sends the plague to the Achaean camp near the beginning of the *Iliad*?

    A. Apollo
    B. Zeus
    C. Hera
    D. Moses

2. When does Achilles die?

    A. In Book 4
    B. In Book 12
    C. In Book 24
    D. He doesn't die in the *Iliad*

3. Which of the following characters do not engage in one-on-one combat with each other in the poem?

    A. Paris and Menelaus
    B. Achilles and Agenor
    C. Hector and Ajax
    D. Priam and Agamemnon

4. When is the *Iliad* thought to have been composed?

    A. The twelfth century B.C.
    B. The fifteenth century B.C.
    C. The eighth century B.C.
    D. The third century B.C.

5. Who helps rescue Machaon after Paris wounds him?

    A. Nestor
    B. Hector
    C. Patroclus
    D. Odysseus

6. Who kills Dolon?

    A.   Odysseus
    B.   Aeneas
    C.   Ajax
    D.   Diomedes

7. With what weapon does Ajax knock Hector unconscious?

    A.   A boulder
    B.   A spear
    C.   A wooden club
    D.   His astonishing good looks

8. At what point in the story do the Achaeans hold their athletic competition?

    A.   After the war
    B.   Before the war
    C.   After the funeral of Patroclus
    D.   When Achilles rejoins the battle

9. Which of the following characters is Helen's brother-in-law?

    A.   Hector
    B.   Achilles
    C.   Agenor
    D.   Agamemnon

10. How long has the Trojan War been going by the time the *Iliad* begins?

    A.   Nine years
    B.   Eight months
    C.   One week
    D.   The poem begins with the beginning of the war

11. How many Trojan warriors does Achilles sacrifice on Patroclus's pyre?

    A.   100
    B.   12
    C.   8
    D.   25

12. Who suggests that Helen be returned to Menelaus?

    A. Hector
    B. Hecuba
    C. Paris
    D. Antenor

13. Who reminds Achilles that the Achaean soldiers cannot fight on empty stomachs?

    A. Ajax
    B. Odysseus
    C. Agamemnon
    D. Menelaus

14. Which god helps to bring about the death of Patroclus?

    A. Zeus
    B. Hephaestus
    C. Poseidon
    D. Apollo

15. Why is Astyanax frightened when he sees his father, Hector?

    A. He sees Hector's blood-stained sword
    B. He foresees Hector's death
    C. The plume on Hector's helmet startles him
    D. He worries that Hector will bring him back to the battlefield with him

16. Which of the following do not appear on Achilles' new shield?

    A. Dancing children
    B. Constellations
    C. Verdant pastures
    D. Valiant warriors

17. With which immortal does Achilles engage in one-on-one combat?

    A. The river god Xanthus
    B. Zeus
    C. Hephaestus
    D. Apollo

18. Why does Zeus initially agree to help the Trojans in the war?

   A.   Because he thinks Paris deserves Helen more than
        Menelaus does
   B.   He does so as a favor to Thetis, who asks him on
        behalf of Achilles
   C.   He does so to spite his nagging wife, Hera
   D.   Because he despises Odysseus for lusting after Hera

19. What provokes Achilles' rage against Agamemnon?

   A.   Agamemnon's demand that Achilles hand over Briseis
   B.   Agamemnon's insults of Achilles' lineage
   C.   Agamemnon's defeat of Achilles in a footrace
   D.   Agamemnon's repeated sending of Achilles to the
        front lines, where the danger of being killed is greatest

20. Who raised Patroclus?

   A.   Thetis
   B.   Peleus
   C.   Shepherds on Mount Ida
   D.   Nestor

21. Who sets fire to a Greek ship?

   A.   Aeneas
   B.   Hephaestus, god of fire and iron
   C.   Hector
   D.   Agamemnon, in a suicidal urge

22. What magical charm does Hera use in seducing Zeus and
    making him fall asleep?

   A.   Some powder from a ground-up rhinoceros horn
   B.   An enchanted breastband from Aphrodite
   C.   A magical potion mixed by the Sirens
   D.   A talisman that Hermes gave her

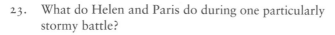

23. What do Helen and Paris do during one particularly stormy battle?

   A. They pray to the gods
   B. They set up an orphanage for the future orphans of Troy
   C. They mix medicines
   D. They sleep together

24. Where is Achilles' old armor most vulnerable to attack?

   A. At the heel
   B. At the elbow
   C. At the neck
   D. In the eye visor

25. What grave tactical error does Hector make out of overconfidence?

   A. He orders his men to put down their swords and fight with daggers
   B. He orders his men to camp outside Troy's walls
   C. He gives permission for half of his men to go on vacation
   D. He decides that his troops do not need to eat before fighting

SUGGESTIONS FOR FURTHER READING

BURKERT, WALTER. *Greek Religion.* Trans. John Raffan. Cambridge, Massachusetts: Harvard University Press, 1987.

CAMPS, W. A. *An Introduction to Homer.* Oxford: Oxford University Press, 1980.

EDWARDS, MARK W. *Homer: Poet of* THE ILIAD. Baltimore: Johns Hopkins University Press, 1987.

GRIFFIN, JASPER. *Homer on Life and Death.* Oxford: Oxford University Press, 1980.

KIRK, G. S. *The Songs of Homer.* Cambridge: Cambridge University Press, 1962.

NAGY, GREGORY. *The Best of the Achaeans: Concepts of the Hero in Archaic Greek Poetry.* Baltimore: Johns Hopkins University Press, 1979.

SILK, M. S. *Homer:* THE ILIAD. Cambridge: Cambridge University Press, 1987.

VIVANTE, PAOLO. *Homer.* New Haven: Yale University Press, 1985.

REVIEW & RESOURCES

SPARKNOTES
TEST PREPARATION
GUIDES

The SparkNotes team figured it was time to cut standardized tests down to size. We've studied the tests for you, so that SparkNotes test prep guides are:

Smarter:
Packed with critical thinking skills and test-
taking strategies that will improve your score.

Better:
Fully up to date, covering all new features of the tests,
with study tips on every type of question.

Faster:
Our books cover exactly what you need to
know for the test. No more, no less.

SparkNotes Guide to the SAT & PSAT
SparkNotes Guide to the SAT & PSAT—Deluxe Internet Edition
SparkNotes Guide to the ACT
SparkNotes Guide to the ACT—Deluxe Internet Edition
SparkNotes Guide to the SAT II Writing
SparkNotes Guide to the SAT II U.S. History
SparkNotes Guide to the SAT II Math Ic
SparkNotes Guide to the SAT II Math IIc
SparkNotes Guide to the SAT II Biology
SparkNotes Guide to the SAT II Physics

SPARKNOTES STUDY GUIDES IN PRINT:

1984
The Adventures of
　Huckleberry Finn
The Adventures of
　Tom Sawyer
The Aeneid
All Quiet on the
　Western Front
And Then There
　Were None
Angela's Ashes
Animal Farm
Anne of Green Gables
Anthem
Antony and Cleopatra
As I Lay Dying
As You Like It
The Awakening
The Bean Trees
The Bell Jar
Beloved
Beowulf
Billy Budd
Black Boy
Bless Me, Ultima
The Bluest Eye
Brave New World
The Brothers
　Karamazov
The Call of the Wild
Candide
The Canterbury Tales
Catch-22
The Catcher in the Rye
The Chosen
Cold Mountain
Cold Sassy Tree
The Color Purple
The Count of
　Monte Cristo
Crime and Punishment
The Crucible
Cry, the Beloved
　Country
Cyrano de Bergerac
David Copperfield
Death of a Salesman
The Diary of a
　Young Girl

Doctor Faustus
A Doll's House
Don Quixote
Dr. Jekyll and Mr. Hyde
Dracula
Dune
Emma
Ethan Frome
Fahrenheit 451
Fallen Angels
A Farewell to Arms
Flowers for Algernon
The Fountainhead
Frankenstein
The Glass Menagerie
Gone With the Wind
The Good Earth
The Grapes of Wrath
Great Expectations
The Great Gatsby
Grendel
Gulliver's Travels
Hamlet
The Handmaid's Tale
Hard Times
Harry Potter and the
　Sorcerer's Stone
Heart of Darkness
Henry IV, Part I
Henry V
Hiroshima
The Hobbit
The House of the
　Seven Gables
I Know Why the
　Caged Bird Sings
The Iliad
Inferno
Invisible Man
Jane Eyre
Johnny Tremain
The Joy Luck Club
Julius Caesar
The Jungle
The Killer Angels
King Lear
The Last of the
　Mohicans
Les Misérables

A Lesson Before
　Dying
The Little Prince
Little Women
Lord of the Flies
The Lord of the Rings
Macbeth
Madame Bovary
A Man for All Seasons
The Mayor of
　Casterbridge
The Merchant of
　Venice
A Midsummer
　Night's Dream
Moby-Dick
Much Ado About
　Nothing
My Ántonia
Mythology
Narrative of the Life of
　Frederick Douglass
Native Son
The New Testament
Night
Notes from
　Underground
The Odyssey
The Oedipus Trilogy
Of Mice and Men
The Old Man and
　the Sea
The Old Testament
Oliver Twist
The Once and
　Future King
One Flew Over the
　Cuckoo's Nest
One Hundred Years
　of Solitude
Othello
Our Town
The Outsiders
Paradise Lost
A Passage to India
The Pearl
The Picture of
　Dorian Gray
Poe's Short Stories

A Portrait of the Artist
　as a Young Man
Pride and Prejudice
The Prince
A Raisin in the Sun
The Red Badge of
　Courage
The Republic
Richard III
Robinson Crusoe
Romeo and Juliet
The Scarlet Letter
A Separate Peace
Silas Marner
Sir Gawain and the
　Green Knight
Slaughterhouse-Five
Snow Falling on Cedars
Song of Solomon
The Sound and the Fury
Steppenwolf
The Stranger
A Streetcar Named
　Desire
The Sun Also Rises
A Tale of Two Cities
The Taming of
　the Shrew
The Tempest
Tess of the
　d'Urbervilles
Their Eyes Were
　Watching God
Things Fall Apart
The Things They
　Carried
To Kill a Mockingbird
To the Lighthouse
Treasure Island
Twelfth Night
Ulysses
Uncle Tom's Cabin
Walden
War and Peace
Wuthering Heights
A Yellow Raft in
　Blue Water